The Life-Changing Power
in the Blood of Christ

BOOKS BY JENNIFER KENNEDY DEAN

FROM NEW HOPE PUBLISHERS

Heart's Cry
The Praying Life
Riches Stored in Secret Places
Legacy of Prayer
Live a Praying Life

THE LIFE-CHANGING POWER IN THE BLOOD OF CHRIST

JENNIFER KENNEDY DEAN

New Hope Publishers

Birmingham, Alabama

New Hope® Publishers
P. O. Box 12065
Birmingham, AL 35202-2065
www.newhopepubl.com

Library of Congress Cataloging-in-Publication Data
Dean, Jennifer Kennedy.
The life-changing power in the blood of Christ / by Jennifer Kennedy Dean.
p. cm.
ISBN 1-56309-753-2
1.   Jesus Christ-Crucifixion. 2. Precious Blood, Devotion to. I.
Title.
BT450.D43 2003
232'.4—dc21
2003002708

Cover design by Identity Design, Dallas, Texas

ISBN: 1-56309-753-2

N034111 • 0603 • 7M1

<u>DEDICATION</u>

To my husband and our sons.

You are my rare and beautiful treasures.
(Proverbs 24:4)

MEET THE AUTHOR

JENNIFER KENNEDY DEAN

Cofounder of the Praying Life Foundation and a leader in the study of prayer and spiritual formation, Jennifer Kennedy Dean is an internationally-known author and conference leader. She conducts seminars around the world—including at Billy Graham's Training Center, the Cove—addressing prayer as a relationship, and she has written numerous magazine articles on prayer and spiritual development.

Her brother's struggle with leukemia and subsequent death were the experiences that ushered Jennifer into a deeper pursuit of prayer. "The question I was left with, despite all my prayer, was: *If he died anyway—what was the point?* That was the beginning of my quest." Jennifer went through many stages in grieving her brother's death, including seeking the everlasting truths she shares in books and seminars today.

"I don't introduce new concepts," Dean notes. "If they were new, they wouldn't be true. I think they sound new to many people because they are aspects of prayer not commonly addressed. I think my strength is to take eternal truths and frame them differently—put them into words and illustrations that cause readers to grasp truths that had seemed remote."

Jennifer lives near Kansas City, Missouri, with her husband, Wayne. The Deans have three college-age sons. Jennifer Kennedy Dean divides her time between speaking engagements, writing articles, and working on her next book. For more information about Jennifer, see www.prayinglife.org.

A WORD FROM THE AUTHOR

Just as the world aims at, strives after, wishes for, craves, and diligently seeks the world's riches, we as kingdom-dwellers must spend that energy and passion diligently seeking kingdom riches. The blood of Christ is the *most* precious commodity, the *most* prized possession, the *most* valued treasure in the kingdom of God. Seek its fullness with all your heart.

I wish I could sit down face to face with you, our Bibles open, and show you these truths one-on-one. I pray that the words you read will not be just words on a page, but the Word from His mouth. I pray that He will speak these truths into the soil of your heart.

This understanding of the blood of Christ has been utterly awe-inspiring to me. I am flooded with love for my Lord and Savior—it overwhelms me. Until I saw the depths in the blood of Christ, I only *thought* I understood how precious I am to Him. I only *thought* I knew how precious He is to me. I pray, my dear friend, that you are as moved as I have been to discover the power of the blood.
—Jennifer Kennedy Dean

CONTENTS

ACKNOWLEDGMENTS

There are numerous people without whose prayers and generous gifts of time and talents there would be no ministry. I can't thank you enough.

Terry and Dung Trieu, Mary and Burley Medley, Joann and K.C. Stokes, Mary Lee Butler, Wanda Kanai, Janelle Lapaglia, Faye Pind, Kaye Walker, Kenny Hiles, Leo Eisert, Ann Whitworth.

May you receive from the Lord's hand a hundred-fold increase on that which you have so freely given into this ministry.

INTRODUCTION

The blood of Christ is the thread that runs through the Bible from beginning to end, tying it together into a comprehensive whole. The blood of Christ flows through every book, every chapter, every verse—sometimes in the foreground, sometimes in the background. It is the central theme. Everything points to it. Surely a fuller understanding of the precious blood is imperative for our spiritual formation. It is the very heartbeat of the living, active Word of God.

One morning as I read a familiar verse—one so familiar that its words almost didn't register—I was suddenly struck with a new thought. I was reading 1 John 1:7, "The blood of Jesus, his Son, purifies us from all sin." I discovered that the tense of the word *purifies* makes it an ongoing action, not a one-time occurrence. The blood of Jesus is purifying me in a sustained, uninterrupted action. *Right now*, as I live my daily life, as I go about my activities, Jesus' blood is acting powerfully to cleanse me. Jesus' blood is making me cleaner and cleaner as each moment passes. If Jesus' blood is actively cleansing me in the present moment, then it has to be near me; it can't be far away from me. Are you seeing this?

I continued reading with awakened curiosity, "If we confess our sins, he is faithful and just and will forgive us our sins and purify us from all unrighteousness" (1 John 1:9). I was further struck with the idea that He not only *forgives our sins*, but He also *purifies us from all unrighteousness*.

The Spirit of God began to stir in me a hunger for more. Does this ever happen to you? There's something about which you think you know all there is to know, but one day you get a little peek under the surface and are astounded to realize that there are depths of understanding and knowledge yet to be mined. Such was my experience that morning with the blood of Christ. I had no idea what was there, but I knew there was something. Here's a little secret about me: I am greedy for the things of the Spirit. I crave them. Once I get the idea there's more, I want it all! Thus began my obsession with the blood of Christ.

In the course of my search, God placed three books in my path. Each introduced me to new thoughts and nudged me in new directions: *In His Image* by Paul Brand and Phillip Yancey, *The Saving Life of Christ* by Major Ian Thomas, and *The Chemistry of the Blood* by M. R. DeHaan. These writers have significantly influenced my approach. If you are familiar with their work, then you will recognize the impact of their thoughts throughout this study.

For many years God has been leading me deeper into the cleansing fountain, unlocking its secrets, amazing me with its wonderful power. I can hardly wait for you to see. I believe that in delving into the riches stored in secret places—the truths once hidden, but now revealed—you will recognize the blood of Christ as the answer to everything you are longing for.

Let me give you notice. This study will be Scripture-rich and will sometimes require you to apply all your brainpower. This will not be baby food. Go over it as many times as you need to. It will be worth your investment. Would you stop right now and ask the Spirit of Truth to guide you into all truth? Would you tell Him that you cannot be satisfied with anything less than *everything* He has to give? Write out your prayer.

LOOK AHEAD

Included in this book are plans for a worship experience that can be the culmination of the study. You might want to look at it now so that you can begin to plan ahead. If you are doing this study with a group, you might want to assign different people responsibilities for planning different aspects of the worship experience. I suggest that you look it over in advance so that preparations can be made that will create an atmosphere of worship on that meeting day.

THE LIFE

DAY ONE

SETTING THE STAGE

Let me lay some groundwork before we bring in the central focus. Let me introduce you to a way of interpreting. For a few moments, set aside the idea of the blood and simply explore this frame of reference. Then we will put the blood into the picture.

One way that God reveals Himself is through His creation.

Read Romans 1:20 and answer the following questions.

How are God's invisible qualities made visible?

Are His invisible qualities hidden and disguised in His creation?

Romans 1:20 says, *"Since the creation of the world God's invisible qualities—his eternal power and divine nature—have been* clearly seen, *being* understood *from what has been made"* (emphasis mine). Look carefully at what Paul said. The qualities of God that you cannot observe directly by using your physical senses can be observed in His creation. The Creator's creation mirrors Him.

Read Psalm 19:1–4 and answer the following questions.

How would you define the words *declare* and *proclaim* as used by the translators of the New International Version? Look at other translations. Look up the words in a dictionary.

What is all creation doing?

"The heavens declare the glory of God; the skies proclaim the work of his hands. Day after day they pour forth speech; night after night they display knowledge. There is no speech or language where their voice is not heard. Their voice goes out into all the earth, their words to the ends of the world" (Psalm 19:1–4). To put it simply, creation is always talking about God. It is boasting about Him and revealing Him. It is explaining Him and making Him obvious.

This goes beyond the obvious fact that an observer of nature would be compelled to conclude that a Creator exists. Paul says that the invisible qualities of God can be *clearly seen* and *understood* in His creation. That which is invisible has become visible in the form of God's creation. Earth is a three-dimensional model of heaven.

Read Hebrews 11:3 and answer the following questions. I am wording these questions based on the New International Version.

How was the universe formed? In other words, what did all created matter come from?

The earth ("that which is seen") was *not* made out of what?

Then, by implication, the earth ("that which is seen") *is* made out of what?

If the earth is "made out of" or "formed from" the Word of God, then is not the earth a manifestation of or a demonstration of the Word that formed it?

"By faith we understand that the universe was formed at God's command, so that what is seen was not made out of what was visible" (Hebrews 11:3).

The universe—the created world; the material creation
was formed—was fitted together; arranged
at God's command—out of; by means of God's voiced word (*rhema*—a word spoken in present-tense)
so that—cause and effect: God's speaking *caused to be* the material world
what is seen—the material creation
was not made out of—was not generated or caused; did not arise from
what was visible—visible, material components

All matter and all the material realm (earth) was caused by God's voiced word (command). Therefore, when God spoke, that which was invisible took on visible form. That which existed in the reality of the spiritual realm (heaven) was manifested in the material realm in a material form.

By *earth* I mean planet earth, the physical creation, material and tangible aspects of life. By *heaven* I mean the spiritual realities of life. These two aspects of reality, heaven and earth, impact one another. Earth is "what is seen" and heaven is "what is unseen" (2 Corinthians 4:18). Heaven and earth—the seen and the unseen, or the material and the spiritual—are two ends of one continuum called "reality." Heaven is more than your eternal home. Heaven is part of your experience right now.

Which existed first, physical reality or spiritual reality? Read the following Scriptures and look for the evidence that the realities of the spiritual realm were in existence before a material realm existed.

Isaiah 14:12–15

Ezekiel 28:12–19

Hebrews 8:5

Exodus 25:40

John 1:1–2

John 17:5

Of course, spiritual reality existed first. The spiritual world had been in existence long before the material world was created. The spiritual world already had a history before earth came to be.

Lucifer had already led his rebellion and been barred from God's throne room when planet earth and its inhabitants were spoken into being (Isaiah 14:12–15; Ezekiel 28:12–19). The tabernacle existed in heaven before God told Moses to make a copy of it on the earth (Hebrews 8:5; Exodus 25:40). The Son existed in heaven before He existed on earth in material form (John 1:1–2; John 17:5).

When God created the earth, He created a material model of the spiritual realities already in existence. Earth is a picture of the spiritual realities that pre-existed it. Earth reality was made out of spirit reality. *"By faith we understand that the universe was formed at God's command, so that what is seen was not made out of what was visible"* (Hebrews 11:3). To state it another way, what we *can see* was made out of what we *can't see*. The Creator spoke His thoughts into earth-forms and the invisible took on visible structure.

Spiritual reality is always the causative agent of material reality. God's command, or God's Word, is invisible. From it came that which is visible. The earth is always "declaring" (putting on display; announcing) the "glory of God" (His invisible qualities).

God's material creation is an allegory to illustrate spiritual reality. God created the earth to be *in every detail* a diagram or a prototype of that which is invisible. The operating principles of the spiritual realm (heaven) are portrayed in creation (earth). It was God's intention and His deliberate, carefully laid-out plan that the earth should teach spiritual truth.

Jesus often pointed to earth to explain heaven. "Look at the grass . . . look at the birds of the air . . . look at the lilies of the field . . . look at the fields of wheat

. . . look at the fig tree . . . ." Or He told parable after parable, opening with "The kingdom of God is like . . . ."

Earth is our visual. God has given us pictures of spiritual truth in His creation. The more we learn about creation, the more clearly we see the pictures.

The spiritual realm is *eternal;* the material realm is *temporary.*

The spiritual realm is the *substance*; the material realm is the *shadow.*

The spiritual realm is the *reality*; the material realm is the *picture.*

In *The Spiritual Disciplines*, Oswald Chambers writes, "All that we see on this earth is symbolic reality. . . . What are we to understand by a symbol? A symbol represents a spiritual truth by means of image or properties of natural things.

All that meets the bodily sense I deem

Symbolical—one mighty Alphabet

For infant minds! And we in this low world,

Placed with our backs to bright Reality,

That we may learn with young, unwounded ken

The Substance from the Shadow!"

We must not mistake shadow for substance. We must not look at the picture and think it the reality. God's creation is pointing us to His reality. A picture of a mountain is not a mountain. However, a picture of a mountain will help you recognize a mountain when you see one.

Creation is, as Chambers says, an alphabet for infant minds. We put the elements together to make a word, then a sentence, then a paragraph. The more we learn about creation, the fuller the revelation of the Creator it proves to be.

The material realm is a shadow of the spiritual realm. When a shadow is cast, the shadow is proof that a reality with substance exists. The reality, the substance, is found in Christ. The earth-shadow proves the existence of spiritual realities.

"So we fix our eyes not on what is seen, but on what is unseen. For what is seen is temporary, but what is unseen is eternal" (2 Corinthians 4:18). Hebrews 11:1 defines faith this way: *"Now faith is being sure of what we hope for and certain of what we do not see."* Everything in the material realm is shadow. Solid substance is in the spiritual realm.

You will have to change your perceptions in order to let the Spirit of Truth show you the reality behind the shadows. Take a moment to solidify in your mind: earth is a picture; heaven is the reality it pictures.

DAY TWO

THE PICTURE OF LIFE: BLOOD

Blood is an earth-substance that God gave us to illustrate a spiritual reality. Earth-blood is a copy or shadow of what true blood means in heaven. God points us to this illustration in His creation by saying, *"For the life of a creature is in the blood . . . the life of every creature is its blood"* (Leviticus 17:11, 14). Blood is the material illustration of a spiritual reality called "life."

Life is in the blood. Look at the earth picture that points us to this reality. Life really is in the blood. Everything your cells need to thrive—the minerals, vitamins, nutrients, oxygen—is delivered to them through your bloodstream. When you eat, the nutrients in your food are absorbed into your bloodstream and delivered to your cells. When you breathe in air, the oxygen is carried by your bloodstream to your cells. Your bloodstream is the delivery system for everything your body needs for life. Your body has no other source for life or power. Life is only in the blood.

Your bloodstream washes away the toxins that your cells release as they work. These are called metabolites, and they are the waste product of metabolism—the working of your body. Your cells also give off carbon dioxide, which is carried by your blood system to your lungs and expelled from your body.

The cells in your body have no other source for nourishment, oxygen, or cleansing except the bloodstream. Any cell that is deprived of blood will die. Life is in the blood. Apart from the blood, there can be no life. As blood flows through your body, old things are passing away and all things are becoming new. As blood flows through your body, it is purifying you of all "un-right-ness." In an ongoing, continuous, ceaseless action, it is cleansing you of anything that will diminish your body's ability to function at its optimum. It is cleansing you and keeping you cleansed.

If your body were working perfectly, every organ in full health, but your blood drained out, your life would be gone. Your life is in your blood.

Consider a raw, unfertilized hen's egg—the kind we eat. When you break open an egg and find streaks of blood present, then you know that the egg has been fertilized and life has started. The evidence is the presence of blood. Life is in the blood.

SHADOW AND SUBSTANCE

Life is in the blood. *"For the life of a creature is in the blood, and I have given it to you to make atonement for yourselves on the altar; it is the blood that makes atonement for one's life"* (Leviticus 17:11).

Since the Scripture points us directly to the blood in a living creature's body as the picture of "life," let's closely examine what we are to clearly see and understand from what He has made.

▼

Read Leviticus 17:11–14. Use the words of Scripture to answer these questions.

Where is a creature's life?

Why did God give us blood?

What is it that makes atonement?

What needs to be atoned for?

Why does blood make atonement?

What has the eternal value—the red, sticky, earth-stuff called blood, or the life it represents?

▲

Where is a creature's life? *"The life of a creature is **in the blood**."*
Why did God give us blood? *"I have given it to you **to make atonement** for yourselves on the altar."*
What is it that makes atonement? *"**It is the blood** that makes atonement."*
Want needs to be atoned for? *"Makes atonement **for one's life**."*
Why does blood make atonement? *Because it is the life.*
What has the eternal value—the red, sticky, earth-stuff called blood, or the life it represents? *The life. "**Because** the life of every creature is its blood. **That is why** I have said to the Israelites, 'You must not eat the blood of any creature, because the life of every creature is its blood; anyone who eats it must be cut off.'"*

Blood's value is not derived from its physical components, but from what it pictures. We have the detailed picture of life in the blood so that we will know *life* when we see it.

Blood is not the earth picture of just any life. Earth-blood is what God created to stand for and picture *the life*.

THE LIFE

In the *cosmos* (the orderly creation; the whole continuum of reality, including both heaven and earth), there is only one Life.

Read the following Scriptures and mark the words and phrases that indicate that there is only one Life.

"In him was life, and that life was the light of men" (John 1:4).

"For as the Father has life in himself, so he has granted the Son to have life in himself" (John 5:26).

"I am the way and the truth and the life" (John 14:6).

"So that they may take hold of the life that is truly life" (1 Timothy 6:19).

"The life appeared; we have seen it and testify to it" (1 John 1:2).

"He who has the Son has life; he who does not have the Son of God does not have life" (1 John 5:12).

All living creatures, including humans, have biological life (*bios*), but Jesus is the only spiritual life (*zoe*), the only eternal life, the only life that is not moving toward death.

In the material realm, science tells us that we cannot define death until we have defined life. Death is the "not life." In the spiritual realm, he who has the Son has life; he who does not have the Son has "not life" (1 John 5:12).

How does the Scripture describe a person who is apart from Christ?

Ephesians 2:1 and 2:5

Ephesians 5:14

Colossians 2:13

In the material realm, scientists divide things into classifications—organic or inorganic; living or non-living. Organisms cannot change classifications. The law of biogenesis says life comes from life. A non-living organism cannot produce a living organism. A rock, for example, will never produce a flower. What is non-living—lifeless—cannot become living. That which is born inorganic is inorganic; that which is born organic is organic. An organism cannot pass from death to life. An organism cannot change its essential nature and become what it is not.

In the spiritual realm, only Jesus is life. Everything else is "flesh"—progressive death. In the spiritual realm, the two classifications are "flesh" or "spirit." That which is born of the flesh is flesh; that which is born of the Spirit is spirit. Only by dying to our old nature and being born again of the Spirit can we move from flesh to spirit, from death to life. In order to change classifications from death to life, a person has to become an entirely new creation (See 2 Corinthians 5:17). Life is only in the Son, so only the Son can impart life. Life must come from life—Spiritual Biogenesis. Only the person who has the Son has life.

Read the following Scriptures and identify the law of spiritual biogenesis—life can only come from life.

John 3:16–18

John 3:36

John 5:24–27; 39–40

John 6:47–59

John 11:25

John 14:6

Bios, biological life, resembles *zoe,* Christ-life. It has the form of life, but it does not have life. In many ways, it has the appearance of life, but it is not life.

C. S. Lewis writes in *Mere Christianity*:

A statue has the shape of a man but it is not alive. In the same way, man has . . . the "shape" or likeness of God, but he has not got the kind of life God has. . . . But life, in this biological sense, is not the same as the life there is in God.

It is only a kind of shadow or symbol of it. . . . When we come to man, . . . we get the most complete resemblance to God which we know of. Man not only lives, but loves and reasons: biological life reaches its highest known level in him.

But what man, in his natural condition, has not got, is Spiritual life— the higher and different sort of life that exists in God . . . In reality, the difference between biological life and spiritual life is so important that I am going to give them two distinct names. The biological sort which comes to us through nature, and which is always tending to run down and decay so that it can only be kept up by incessant subsidies from nature in the form of air, water, food, etc., is *bios*. The spiritual life which is in God from all eternity, and which made the whole natural universe, is *zoe*. *Bios* has, to be sure, a certain shadowy or symbolic resemblance to *zoe*; but only the sort of resemblance there is between a photo and a place, or a statue and a man. A man who changed from having *bios* to having *zoe* would have gone through as big a change as a statue which changed from being a carved stone to being a real man.

Jesus is the life. Life does not exist apart from Him. Everything else that passes for life in the earth realm is really death in disguise. Why? Because at its outset it has only one possible outcome—death.

We are born with an Adam-life, which is sin-diseased and infected with unrighteousness. The Adam-life, which flows through our spirit-veins, carries death. Adam-life, then, is really death; Adam-life is, in reality, "not life." Death is an active force that works in Adam's race to produce fruit, just as life works in the children of God to produce fruit. The fruit produced through a person is the evidence of either life or death. Death is more than the absence of life; it is a power that operates in and through a person who is without Christ.

Read the following Scriptures and look for the descriptions of death as an active, working force that produces fruit.

Matthew 7:16–20

Romans 7:5

Romans 5:14

You will find that it is important to have a scriptural understanding of death so that you will have a fuller understanding of life. Death is not passive, but active and forceful. It is a power. Life and death cannot co-exist.

DAY THREE

THE SPIRITUAL GENETIC CODE

We have made such strides in understanding our physical genetic makeup that it is now possible to test your DNA and determine that you carry the gene that will produce certain diseases, for example, cancer. Even before a single cancer cell has developed, before a single symptom has manifested itself in your body, you are predisposed to develop the disease.

In the same way, your spiritual DNA structure carries the sin gene. You have inherited Adam's spiritual genetic code (Genesis 5:3). You are born a sinner, not because you are responsible for someone else's sin, but because you are certain to sin. *"Sin entered the world through one man, and death through sin, and in this way death came to all men, because all sinned"* (Romans 5:12). You are born under a death sentence because you are sure to sin. *"The mind of sinful man is death"* (Romans 8:6).

Existence outside Jesus is a steady march toward death. Only through Him can we *"[pass] from death to life"* (1 John 3:14). His life is the only life that exists in all creation. The law of spiritual biogenesis says that life can only come from Him because only Christ is life, and life can only come from life.

Where is His life? *In His blood!*

THE LIFE OPERATING IN ME

"Then the Jews began to argue sharply among themselves, 'How can this man give us his flesh to eat?' Jesus said to them, 'I tell you the truth, unless you eat the flesh of the Son of Man and drink his blood, you have no life in you. Whoever eats my flesh and drinks my blood has eternal life, and I will raise him up on the last day. For my flesh is real food and my blood is real drink. Whoever eats my flesh and drinks my blood remains in me, and I in him.'" —John 6:52–56

Jesus shocked His listeners with these statements. *"On hearing it, many of his disciples said, 'This is a hard teaching. Who can accept it?'"* (John 6:60).

The words are somewhat jarring to our ears, but they were even more so to His Jewish audience. They understood Him to be speaking metaphorically. Such metaphor was a typical teaching device for Jewish rabbis. However, one of the most important injunctions in their religion was, "Don't eat the blood. The blood is the life." Here was Jesus, that outrageous teacher, saying, "Drink My blood. My blood is real drink. Unless you drink My blood, you have no life in you." This was so controversial that it was the beginning of the falling away of many of His followers. *"From this time many of his disciples turned back and no longer followed him"* (John 6:66).

What did Jesus want us to understand? Why did He make this unsettling statement? He is saying: "My life must be inside you. My life must be flowing through your spirit-veins." His life cannot impart life to us from outside. He must be in us. Drawing upon the best biological understanding of His times, Jesus drew a graphic word-picture of how that which is outside of you can be inside of you: eating and drinking. If He were drawing the picture using twenty-first century concepts, He might have used the picture of blood transfusion. He wants to transfuse us with His life.

M. R. DeHaan, in his book *The Chemistry of the Blood*, says the following:

To redeem this DEAD sinner, life must be again imparted. The only remedy for death is LIFE. This life is in the blood, so a blood must be furnished which is sinless and incorruptible. Now none of Adam's race could do this. For *in Adam all died. All have sinned and come short.* The angels could not furnish that blood for they are spirit beings and have neither flesh nor blood. There was only one, yes ONLY ONE, who could furnish that blood: the virgin-born Son of God, with a human body, but sinless supernatural blood, inseminated by the Holy Ghost . . . death can only be banished by life. A blood transfusion must be performed and provided . . . the greatest of all transfusions is performed, when a poor sinner, dead in trespasses and in sins, is transfused by the blood of Christ the moment he believes.

Just as blood flows through your physical veins, His life, His blood in its spiritual form, flows through your spirit-veins. Your physical body is a picture, a shadow, of your spirit. Just as your natural earth-body is given life through blood, so your spirit-body has life through the blood of Christ.

Look with me in Scripture to see that your physical body mirrors your spirit. Read the following Scriptures. Notice the reference to physical body parts. Yet in each case, is the Scripture referring to a physical body or to a spiritual reality?

Romans 5:5

Romans 16:20; Ephesians 6:15

2 Samuel 10:6

Psalm 119:103

Ephesians 1:18

Isaiah 50:5

Each of your body's parts and each of your physical senses corresponds to an eternal reality about how your spirit operates. For your earth-body, life is in the blood. For your spirit, life is in the blood.

Now, I want to take you to the next step in bringing this picture into sharp focus. Tomorrow we start looking at what the Scripture shows us about the beautiful, beautiful life that is in the blood.

DAY FOUR

THE LIFE IN THE BLOOD

Jesus' blood has two roles in our salvation. As the study progresses, you will identify two problems for which we need a Savior, and you will clearly see that Jesus' blood takes care of both problems. Right now, you need to see that the blood has a two-fold role in our salvation.

Read Romans 5:10 and answer the following questions.

What reconciled us to the Father?

What does it mean to be "reconciled to the Father"?

What saves us on an ongoing basis?

What does it mean to be "being saved"?

▲

"We were reconciled to him through the death of his Son (a completed action), *how much more, having been reconciled* (a finished work), *shall we be saved* (an ongoing, continuous action) *through his life"* (Romans 5:10, material in parentheses added). We are reconciled through His death, but we are saved by His life. This concept is the basis for the book *The Saving Life of Christ* by Major Ian Thomas, and it has profoundly affected my understanding of the blood.

We have two problems for which we need a Savior: (1) the sins we commit, and (2) the unrighteousness that causes us to commit them. Jesus' blood takes care of both problems. His blood has two roles in your salvation:
• His earth-blood that He spilled out for payment of sin: *"We were reconciled to him through the death of his Son . . ."*
• His Spirit-blood, His life, that He poured out before the Father in the heavenly tabernacle and that now runs through your spirit-veins, cleansing you of the unrighteousness that causes you to sin: *"How much more, having been reconciled, shall we be saved through his life!"*

THE BLOOD'S TWO-FOLD ROLE

We are reconciled to the Father through the *death* of the Son, but we are saved by the *life* of the Son. Our salvation has two components: (1) what Christ did for us, and (2) who Christ is in us.

We have a two-fold solution for a two-fold problem.

		Unrighteousness that causes us to sin
PROBLEM	Sins we commit	
SOLUTION	Reconciled by His death; what Christ did for us	Saved by His life; who Christ is in us
PROMISE	Forgive our sins	Purify us of all unrighteousness

The earth-blood that ran through the veins of the earth-body of Jesus was made up of the same physical components that make up your blood and my blood. It was made up of red cells and white cells and platelets. *"Since the children have flesh and blood, he too shared in their humanity so that by his death he might destroy him who holds the power of death . . . . For this reason he had to be made like his brothers in every way, in order that he might become a merciful and faithful high priest in service to God, and that he might make atonement for the sins of the people"* (Hebrews 2:14, 17). What made His blood precious? What made it priceless? What made it like no other blood ever created? What made it acceptable as payment for sin? Because it was the shadow and picture of His life. His life imparted the value to His blood. Because not one drop of sin's infection invaded His life, His blood was deemed pure. His earth-blood differed from ours in that it had no Adam-effect in it. Unlike our blood, His earth-blood did not have disease and death in it because He had no inheritance from Adam, a concept we will explore in detail later in the study. But its chemical, molecular, physical makeup was the blood of a man.

Did the Life (Jesus) exist before He was born on earth as a man? Read John 1:1–3, 1 John 1:1, Hebrews 1:2, and Colossians 1:15–17.

Did the body in which He lived—in which He was born, died on the cross, and was buried—exist before Jesus was born on the earth? Read Hebrews 10:5.

If the physical body that housed the Life did not exist until Jesus came to earth in the form of man, then did the physical blood that ran through that body exist before His incarnation?

Do you agree with this conclusion: *The Life—the true blood—is eternal and has always been. The physical blood in the physical body of Jesus was blood that ran through a human body and did not exist until Jesus was born on the earth.* Yes or no?

I believe the evidence will point you squarely to one conclusion: the precious, one-of-a kind, perfectly pure blood that ran through the earth-veins of the earth-body of Jesus was an exact picture of His life. It perfectly, beautifully pictured an eternal reality.

When Jesus, our atonement sacrifice, died on a cross outside of Jerusalem, every last drop of His earth-blood spilled out. He poured out every red blood cell, every white blood cell, every platelet from His dear body to pay for the sins I commit so that He could reconcile me to the Father through His death. His death was designed before the world was formed to be a certain kind of death—a death that would pour out His blood. *It is the blood* that makes atonement for our lives. It is not the death, but the blood. The death is the means by which the blood was poured out. When His body died, the totality of Scripture indicates that it was because He had bled to death.

This was all laid out in picture-form in the Old Testament. In the Old Testament, it was required for a blood sacrifice that all the blood be drained from the animal. It cost a whole life—every last drop—to atone for a life. Each time the ritual for a blood sacrifice is detailed, it ends with all the blood being poured out at the base of the altar. The word often translated "poured out" is actually the Hebrew word *shaphak*, which means "dashed, thrown, splashed." It hints at pouring out with vigor, force, or violence, not just dribbled out. The Greek equivalent, *ekcheo*, was used by Jesus when He said that His blood would be "poured out" (Luke 22:20). Harkening to the perceptions and nuances of His audience, He was saying that *all of His blood* would be dashed against the base of the altar.

In the Old Testament, on the Day of Atonement, the High Priest dipped his finger into the blood of the atonement sacrifice and sprinkled it once upward and seven times downward. The blood of our sacrifice was sprinkled on earth seven times:

1. When He sweat drops of blood (Luke 22:44).
2. When they plucked out His beard and beat His face (Luke 22:63–64; John 19:3; Mark 14:65; Matthew 26:67–68; Isaiah 50:6).
3. When they placed the crown of thorns on His head and beat His head (Matthew 27:29–30).
4. When His back was scourged (Matthew 27:26).
5. When His hands were pierced (John 20:20, 25, 27; Psalm 22:16).
6. When His feet were pierced (Luke 24:38–39; Psalm 22:16).
7. When His side was pierced (John 19:34).

Jesus was both the High Priest offering the sacrifice and the sacrifice being offered. He offered Himself (Hebrews 7:27, 9:14). His earth-blood, made out of earth-stuff, which ran through His earth-body, was *all poured out* at the cross for the forgiveness of sins. It was all dashed against the base of the altar.

We were reconciled to God through the death of His Son—through His earth-blood shed on the cross.

After He, the Eternal High Priest, had offered Himself as the atonement for our sins, He then entered into the Tabernacle in heaven, there to offer His blood on the Mercy Seat. *"When Christ came as high priest of the good things that are already here, he went through the greater and more perfect tabernacle that is not man-made, that is to say, not a part of this creation. He did not enter by means of the blood of goats and calves; but he entered the Most Holy Place once for all by his own blood, having obtained eternal redemption"* (Hebrews 9:11–12).

How does the Scripture identify the tabernacle into which Jesus entered?

What tabernacle did He *not* enter into?

What did He take into the tabernacle?

What did He *not* take into the tabernacle?

Into what tabernacle did Jesus enter? Into the tabernacle on earth—the shadow and copy? Or into the real tabernacle—the substance and reality? Read the words again: *"He went through the greater and more perfect tabernacle that is not man-made, that is to say, not a part of this creation."* He went into the real tabernacle. The writer goes to some lengths to make the point that there is a shadow tabernacle and there is a real tabernacle and that Jesus had no use for the shadow version.

He took into the real tabernacle, not the blood of goats and bulls, but *His own blood.*

Consider this: Where did Jesus get the blood? Remember that His earth-blood all drained out at the cross. Did Jesus go back down to earth and scoop up the red sticky earth-stuff called blood and bring it into the true tabernacle? Of course not. He did not take the shadow; He took the substance. He did not offer His earth-blood in the Most Holy Place. He offered His life, the eternal blood.

When Jesus entered the eternal tabernacle with His own blood, what was the container that held His blood? In the Old Testament, the High Priest carried the blood of the sacrifice in a copper vessel. Did Jesus have a copper vessel full of His own blood? No. Jesus is the copper vessel. He contained His own life. His blood is not something separate from Him. His life is in His blood; His blood is in His person; and His person is in us. Christ in you is your hope of glory.

His earth-blood flowed through an earth-body. It was made of earth-stuff. In no way does this demean the inestimable value, the complete holiness, the unutterable worth of the blood that ran through His earth-body. It perfectly mirrored His life. It was flawless. It had none of the effects of sin that we have in our earth blood—diseases, aging, defects, deficiencies. It was perfect blood. It was precious blood.

Remember, before the Incarnation, when the Word became flesh, Jesus did not have an earth-body. He did not have earth-blood. But the Life has always been. When the beginning came, the Word already was (John 1:1). His earth-blood was a copy and a picture of the Life that has always been and will always be.

In the Book of Revelation we are given a glimpse into the spiritual realm. The Spirit of God describes for us a reality that is invisible to us from the earth. *"And he said, 'These are they who have come out of the great tribulation; they have washed their robes and made them white in the blood of the Lamb'"* (Revelation 7:14). When they washed their robes in the blood, their robes became white. Now let me ask you to consider this: if a person had taken his robe and washed it in the blood of Jesus that flowed from His body on the cross, would that person's robe have become white? I think you will have to agree that the precious blood that flowed from His earth-body stained everything it touched with the red color of His blood. But the eternal blood washes white as snow.

His spirit-blood has no earthly limitations. His spirit-blood is Spirit-life. The power of the Father flows through the life (blood) of the Son. The fullness of God is in Jesus (Colossians 1:19). Just like earth-blood is the delivery system for everything your body needs to thrive, so the life of the Son is the delivery system for everything you need to thrive spiritually. *"His divine power has given us everything we need for life and godliness through our knowledge of him who called us by his own glory and goodness"* (2 Peter 1:3).

What happened to the blood He poured out in the true tabernacle? *"On that day a fountain will be opened to the house of David and the inhabitants of Jerusalem, to cleanse them from sin and impurity"* (Zechariah 13:1). Jesus' blood became a flowing fountain rather than a stagnant pool. The life, His blood in its Spirit-form, continues to stream from His veins, covering and filling everyone who comes to Him. John, in his Revelation of heaven, saw the Lamb on the throne looking as if He had just been slain. *"Then I saw a Lamb, looking as if it had been slain, standing in the center of the throne, encircled by the four living creatures and the elders"* (Revelation 5:6). Don't you think that must mean that the blood was flowing from Him? The fountain of His blood flows through you and me to cleanse us from sin and impurity and to bring us perpetual newness of life. He is the fountain, and the fountain is filled with the life: *"For with you is the fountain of life"* (Psalm 36:9). *"In that day . . . . A fountain will flow out of the Lord's house"* (Joel 3:18).

The blood that Jesus poured out in the heavens flows through you now. His blood in Spirit-form flows from heaven's mercy seat, from the veins of the Living Lord Jesus, through you. You are transfused with His life.

The ever-flowing blood of Jesus is the delivery system for God's power. The power works in the blood. His life, His blood in Spirit-form, flows through you like blood flows through your body.

There is a fountain filled with blood
Drawn from Immanuel's veins;
And sinners, plunged beneath that flood,
Lose all their guilty stains.

E'er since by faith I saw the stream
Thy flowing wounds supply,
Redeeming love has been my theme,
And shall be till I die.

—"There Is a Fountain" by William Cowper

DAY FIVE

THE LIFE APPEARED

John writes, *"The life appeared; we have seen it and testify to it"* (1 John 1:2). For a period of time His life was contained in an earth-body that God had prepared for Him: *"But a body you prepared for me"* (Hebrews 10:2). His life was something separate from His body, but was contained in and expressed through His body. During that period of time His work was limited to that one and only physical vehicle. When that earth-vehicle was destroyed, the life it contained was no longer limited to one body.

The life that for a time—a moment in history—was contained in the earth-body that was born in Bethlehem and died on a cross outside Jerusalem is now in my body and in your body and in the body of each believer. Now His life operates on earth through my earth-body. When Jesus finished with his earth-body, the way was opened for His life to indwell the earth-bodies of His followers; for His blood in Spirit-form to flow through our spirit-veins.

God shows us this truth in a picture He placed on the earth. Every object in the temple was a shadow or copy of a solid reality that exists in the spiritual realm. The writer of Hebrews explains that Jesus' earth-body was the reality pictured by the temple veil that separated the Holy of Holies from the rest of the temple. It hid the presence of God. He writes: *"a new and living way opened for us through the curtain, that is, his body"* (Hebrews 10:20).

When the real veil, His earth-body, was destroyed, the shadow veil was destroyed at the same moment. *"And when Jesus had cried out again in a loud voice, he gave up his spirit. At that moment the curtain in the temple was torn in two from top to bottom"* (Matthew 27:50–51). The presence of God—the Life—was no longer limited to a single earth-body. The Life was made available for all who would receive the blood transfusion.

The ever-flowing blood of Jesus fills me with the Life. I must trust His life operating in me. His life—His thoughts, His desires, His wisdom and understanding—are being expressed through a vehicle I call "Jennifer." I no longer live, but Christ lives in me!

THE TWO-FOLD FUNCTION OF THE BLOOD

Not only does the blood have two roles in my salvation, but the blood of Christ also has two functions in my life: *"The blood of Jesus, his Son, purifies us from all sin. . . . If we confess our sins, he is faithful and just and will forgive us our sins and purify us from all unrighteousness"* (1 John 1:7, 9).

Jesus Himself lives in and through me. His life flows through me like blood flows through my body. The Scripture says, *"The blood of Jesus, his Son, purifies us from all sin"* (1 John 1:7). How does blood purify? It purifies from the inside. Blood does not cleanse by being applied externally. It cleanses only as it flows through. As blood flows through my body, its red cells absorb toxins and transport them to the organs through which they will be expelled. My blood cleanses me continually *as it flows through me*.

The life of Jesus, Jesus Himself, flows through me. His blood in Spirit-form flows from heaven's Mercy Seat through me. The Scripture tells us that when we confess our sins, two things happen: (1) He forgives us our sins, and (2) He purifies us from all unrighteousness. That fountain, Zechariah said, is for cleansing from both *sin* (the sinful actions we engage in) and *impurity* (the unrighteousness that causes us to sin). In Isaiah 53:5 we read, *"He was pierced for our transgressions, he was crushed for our iniquities."* The word for "transgressions" (*pesha*) means "rebellion or revolt"—the attitude that produces the act; the word for "iniquities" (*avon*) means "mischief, behavior, fault"—the actions of sin we commit. He died for both our rebellious attitude and the sins that it produces.

From the following Scriptures, identify the words or phrases that assure us that both problems—sin and unrighteousness—have been settled.

Romans 5:10

Romans 6:5

1 John 1:9

Isaiah 53:2

Hebrews 5:1–6; 7:1–17

Hebrews 1:3

SCRIPTURE	SINS/ death of Christ	UNRIGHTEOUSNESS/ life of Christ
Romans 5:10	Reconciled through the death of His son	Saved through His life
Romans 6:5	United with Him in His death	United with Him in His resurrection
Romans 6:10	The death He died, He died to sin	The life He lives, He lives to God
1 John 1:9	Forgive our sins	Purify us from all unrighteousness
Isaiah 53:5	Crushed for our iniquities	Pierced for our transgressions
Hebrews 5:1–6; 7:1–17	Jesus: priest after the order of Aaron—to offer sacrifice on the altar to atone for sins	Jesus: priest after the order of Melchizedeck— "on the basis of an indestructible life"
Hebrews 1:3	Provided purification for sins (died on the cross)	Sat down at the right hand of the majesty on high (lives and rules eternally)

God will both forgive our sins—we are reconciled by His death; and He will purify the unrighteousness that causes us to sin—we are saved by His life.

"Having our hearts sprinkled to cleanse us from a guilty conscience" (Hebrews 10:22). If the blood is being sprinkled upon our hearts and is cleansing our conscience, then where does the blood have to be?

You have the very life of Jesus, the delivery system for all the power of God, flowing through you. What does God have to give you? Nothing but the blood of Jesus!

REFLECT

Sit quietly and feel His blood flowing through you. Feel its cleansing power. Feel the energizing effects as His life flows into your thoughts, into your emotions, into your memories. Feel it washing away the toxins of fear, anxiety, guilt, anger, bitterness, disappointment . . . all being washed away by the blood of the Lamb.

Reflect on the words of the classic hymn in the light of new understanding:

What can wash away my sin?
Nothing but the blood of Jesus;
What can make me whole again?
Nothing but the blood of Jesus.

For my pardon, this I see,
Nothing but the blood of Jesus;
For my cleansing, this my plea,
Nothing but the blood of Jesus.

Nothing can for sin atone,
Nothing but the blood of Jesus;
Naught of good that I have done,
Nothing but the blood of Jesus.

This is all my hope and peace,
Nothing but the blood of Jesus;
This is all my righteousness,
Nothing but the blood of Jesus.

Oh! Precious is the flow
That makes me white as snow;
No other fount I know,
Nothing but the blood of Jesus.

—"Nothing but the Blood" by Robert Lowry

Write out your thoughts to Him. Tell Him what it means to you that He has reconciled you by His death and is saving you by His life

_____

_____

THE
ETERNAL LIFE

DAY ONE

I know that the material you covered last week was intensive. Today I want you just to take time to let it settle. I always find that when I am thinking through and meditating on complex thoughts, my mind is sorting, categorizing, filing, and comparing new thoughts to old; and it is doing all this at a different level of consciousness—like a program running in the background, doing work I don't even know it is doing. The result is that after a few days have passed, I find that new thoughts and concepts have taken on substance and I understand them and have words for them.

Today's material might feel like a review, but the purpose is not to see if you remember your lesson. Rather, I want to give you the opportunity to discover that some new thoughts have made a home for themselves in your heart.

The material you covered last week is foundational to this whole study. You need to feel confident that you have absorbed the essence of it. The rest of the study will build on it and add to it.

What do you understand the word "heaven" to mean?

What do you understand the word "earth" to mean?

What is the relationship between heaven and earth?

Which realm of reality, heaven or earth, is solid reality and substance and which is shadow and picture?

Where in creation did the Creator paint a picture of "life"?

What does the picture of "life" cause us to recognize about "life"?

How would you define "death" in the context of defining "life"?

Why is Jesus the only Life in all the cosmos?

Why is Adam's race born with death running through their spirit-veins?

How can a person move from death to life?

Paul writes, *"The gift of God is eternal life in Christ Jesus our Lord"* (Romans 6:23). Where is the life God gives us as a gift?

Where is the blood of Jesus right now?

Jesus is the life. Apart from Him, only death, or the "not life," flows through spirit-veins. He who has the Son has life; he who does not have the Son has "not life."

Let me show you a picture. My brother, Roger, died of leukemia when he was 17 years old. Death was in his blood. Instead of carrying life and cleansing from cell to cell and from organ to organ, Roger's blood carried death and disease. His body had no other source for power and life.

I remember when he was first diagnosed. The very first step in his treatment was to give him a transfusion of healthy blood. A call went out through our community that Roger needed blood. The Red Cross set up a bloodmobile in our church basement and people waited in line for the opportunity to give their healthy blood to replace his diseased blood. Through the miracle of blood transfusion, the very blood that ran through my veins could, temporarily, replace the death-carrying blood that ran through his veins. My life could be in him—just for a moment. And for that short time that my life was in him, it overcame his death. This is what Jesus is longing to do. He is longing to transfuse His life into you to replace the "not life" that flows through you.

Read Romans 5:12. How did death enter the world?

Who inherited death?

Because you are a descendant of Adam, you were born with the sin disease. In Romans 5:12 we read that *"sin entered the world through one man, and death through sin, and in this way death came to all men, because all sinned."* Imagine that from my father I had inherited a genetic disorder that would mean my certain death. I might say, "Death came into my world through one man." Then imagine that I had passed that same fatal disorder on to my children, who passed it on to their children. Generations down the line, my descendants would still be saying, "Death came to me through one man."

You were born in the line of Adam. Your spirit-veins should have been carrying life, but instead they were carrying death. Jesus has opened His veins and poured out His life so that He can flow through you.

In Roger's case, the blood transfusion was only a stop-gap measure. His body continued to produce diseased blood. Only while the healthy blood flowed in his veins were his disease's effects slowed. Soon the "not life" filled his veins again. But Jesus' transfusion is different. It is eternal.

SPIRIT MARROW

Where is my blood manufactured? It is manufactured in my bone marrow. My bone marrow, a spongy substance in the center of my bones, is continually manufacturing blood cells. When they are fully formed, they migrate from my marrow into my bloodstream through a system of specially designed veins. They become part of my bloodstream and begin their work of bringing life and cleansing. As one blood cell is used up—when it has done all it can do—the body sloughs it off and it is immediately replaced by a new, fresh blood cell.

My bone marrow will only manufacture my life. Every single blood cell my marrow creates has my DNA structure in it. My bone marrow will not manufacture any life but Jennifer-life.

There will be a complete turnover of blood cells in my body over the course of three months. Three months from now, not one single blood cell that is in my body right now will still exist. Yet if you were to draw blood from me today and again three months from now, both blood samples, subjected to DNA testing, would prove to be Jennifer-life. Nothing I can do will make my bone marrow stop manufacturing Jennifer-life and start manufacturing some other kind of life. Every Jennifer-cell that is sloughed away is replaced by another Jennifer-cell.

When you were born, your spirit-marrow was manufacturing Adam-life. Your spirit-marrow could not manufacture any other kind of life. No matter how many good deeds you did, no matter how regularly you attended church or how many verses of Scripture you memorized, your spirit marrow could only manufacture Adam-life, the "not life." Death was in your blood. "As for you, you were dead in your transgressions and sins, in which you used to live when you followed the ways of this world and of the ruler of the kingdom of the air, the spirit who is now at work in those who are disobedient" (Ephesians 2:1–2). Your Adam-DNA, the death-gene, was being multiplied in you.

In the physical realm, if I want my bone marrow to manufacture something other than Jennifer-life, there is only one hope. I would have to die and then be born again. In the physical realm, it is not possible. But in the spiritual realm, that is exactly what has occurred. I have died to my Adam-heritage and been born again of the Spirit.

Look carefully at the following Scriptures and underline words and phrases that tell you that you have died to your old nature or that tell you that you have been born again with a completely new nature.

"For we know that our old self was crucified with him so that the body of sin might be done away with, that we should no longer be slaves to sin—because anyone who has died has been freed from sin" (Romans 6:6–7).

"So, my brothers, you also died to the law through the body of Christ, that you might belong to another, to him who was raised from the dead, in order that we might bear fruit to God" (Romans 7:4–5).

"Yet to all who received him, to those who believed in his name, he gave the right to become children of God—children born not of natural descent, nor of human decision or a husband's will, but born of God" (John 1:12–13).

"For you have been born again, not of perishable seed, but of imperishable, through the living and enduring word of God" (1 Peter 1:23).

When I die to my Adam-nature and am born again of the Spirit, I no longer have Adam-life; I have Jesus-life. *"I have been crucified with Christ and **I no longer live**, but **Christ lives in me**. The life I live in the body, I live by faith in the Son of God, who loved me and gave himself for me"* (Galatians 2:20).

In this statement, Paul is saying: "My spirit-marrow no longer manufacturers Adam-life. In fact, that Paul—the Paul who had death running through his spirit veins—is dead. The Paul who was an offspring of Adam no longer exists. I am a completely new creation with a new spiritual DNA structure. Now my spirit-marrow manufactures Jesus-life. The life that runs through my spirit-veins is the blood of Jesus. My body is no longer filled with Adam-life. The life I live in this body is Jesus' life in me—His blood running through me."

Look again at Paul's word from Romans 6:6–7: *"For we know that our old self was crucified with him so that the body of sin might be done away with, that we should no longer be slaves to sin—because anyone who has died has been freed from sin."* He says that the *body of sin*, or the *body of death* (Romans 7:24), has already been done away with. Yet you have the same body now that you had before you were given eternal life. How can Paul say that the body of sin and the body of death have been done away with? I wrote about this briefly in my book, *He Restores My Soul:*

He says that when my old self is crucified, "the body of sin" is "done away with." What is he saying? When he uses the phrase "body of sin," he means the body (the vehicle through which we perform) that belongs to sin; the body through which the old nature acts. When I enter into the crucifixion of Jesus, I do not get a new earth-body. I look just the same as I did before. But now that same old body has been made new internally. Now it no longer contains death; now it contains life. Think of it like this: my computer is encased in an outer structure. When I look at my computer, I see its casing. That's how I recognize it as my computer. However, what really makes my computer my computer is its inner workings. If I were to take my computer to a technician and ask him take out the old computer and put in an entirely new computer, but keep the outer structure, when I take the computer home, I now have a brand new computer. It looks the same to my eyes, but it is a brand new creation. It has a new operating system; it runs new programs; it responds to different commands than before. When Christ comes to be my life, my body is no longer a body of sin. It is now a body of righteousness because the body of sin has been done away with.

Paul says that the transformation is so drastic, so radical, that his body, once a container of death, is now a container of life. The "body of death" has been done away with.

In the physical realm, "life" is an interaction with your environment. If your body is alive, it is breathing air, eating food, responding to the information gathered by its senses. Death is the "not life." A body that is dead does not respond to its environment. It does not feel hunger or cold. The environment has no pull.

In the spiritual realm, a person who is filled with death is alive to the pull or influence of sin. That person, though, is dead to the influence of righteousness. That person cannot feel the pull of God on his or her life. You might say that he is alive to sin, but dead to God.

What happens, then, when a person crosses over *"from death to life"* (John 5:24)? What is the difference?

What does it mean to be *"dead to sin but alive to God in Christ Jesus"* (Romans 6:11)?

DAY THREE

ETERNAL LIFE

What kind of life is Jesus? He is eternal life. *"The life appeared; we have seen it and testify to it, and we proclaim to you the eternal life, which was with the Father and has appeared to us"* (1 John 1:2). *"And we are in him who is true—even in his Son Jesus Christ. He is the true God and eternal life"* (1 John 5:20).

Eternal life is a completely new life—the life of Jesus. It is not an addendum tacked on to my earth-life. Eternal life is not something God gives me apart from Himself. He is eternal life and He is in me. When He transfused me with His life, at that very moment I received eternal life. I'm living it right now. Some day I will live my eternal life without the limits of an earth-body, but the life with be the same. *"The gift of God is eternal life **in Christ Jesus** our Lord"* (Romans 6:23). *"God has given us eternal life, and this life is **in his Son**"* (1 John 5:11).

Jesus said, *"I tell you the truth, whoever hears my word and believes him who sent me **has eternal life** and will not be condemned; **he has crossed over from death to life**. I tell you the truth, a time is coming and **has now come** when the dead will hear the voice of the Son of God and those who hear will live. For as* *the Father has life in himself, so he has granted the Son to have life **in himself**"* (John 5:24–26).

Here's what He's saying: "The time has come when those with death running through their spirit-veins will hear and respond to the voice of the Son, and they will be made alive. They will have eternal life. They will cross from death to life. Why? Because the Son has life in Himself—eternal life. And He has come to live that eternal life in those who believe."

ETERNAL LIFE IS ALWAYS NEW

The word *eternal* means that it has no ending, but also that it has no beginning. *Eternal* means "always has been and always will be." Is there any life that could be called eternal except the life of Jesus?

---▼---

According to Scripture, was there ever a time when the Life did not exist? Will there be a time in the future when the Life will not exist?

*"**In the beginning** was the Word, and the Word was with God, and the Word was God. He was with God in the beginning. Through him all things were made; without him nothing was made that has been made. **In him was life**, and that life was the light of men."* —John 1:1–4

*"For **by him all things were created**: things in heaven and on earth, visible and invisible, whether thrones or powers or rulers or authorities; all things were created by him and for him. **He is before all things**, and in him all things hold together."* —Colossians 1:16–17

"He said to me: 'It is done. I am the Alpha and the Omega, the Beginning and the End.'" —Revelation 21:6

---▲---

When you received Jesus Christ as your personal Savior, His life replaced your death. A radical transaction occurred. Hear this. Really hear it: *you no longer live*, but Christ lives in you. His eternal life is in you. Right this minute, you are living eternal life. You have all the eternal life you are ever going to have. You are living eternal life in the context of earth and time. What was Jesus doing when He lived in an earth-body for 33 years? He was living eternal life in the context of earth and time.

Since eternal life does not grow feeble with the passage of time, does not wear out with use, eternal life is always "now." Eternal life is always new. Paul writes that our life in Christ is the *"newness of life"* (Romans 6:4 NASB). We are always walking in "newness."

Looking again at the earth-picture, you realize that your bone marrow is continually creating new blood cells. Old blood cells are passing away and new blood cells are taking their place in any ongoing process. You are always being newly created. You are not the same today as you were yesterday; nor will you be the same tomorrow as you are today.

In the material realm, everything that starts off new begins immediately to grow old. At some point, your body stops manufacturing fresh cells fast enough to replace old, used-up cells. But eternal life is forever new. It starts out new and stays new. It is eternal. You become "new-er" every day. *"Though outwardly we are wasting away, yet inwardly we are being renewed day by day"* (2 Corinthians 4:16). We walk in perpetual newness. Today, you are not what you will be tomorrow. In fact, *"it has not appeared as yet what we will be"* (1 John 3:2 NASB). This process of ever-increasing renewal, this ongoing rejuvenation, continues until the very moment you leave your earth-body behind.

Your spirit veins have some left-over, residual Adam-life flowing through them. But as an Adam-cell is sloughed off, it is not replaced by another Adam-cell. It is replaced by a Jesus-cell. Little by little, that Adam-life—your flesh—is dying off and being replaced by eternal life. You are *"being transformed into his likeness with ever-increasing glory, which comes from the Lord, who is the Spirit"* (2 Corinthians 3:18). You are getting new-er.

DAY FOUR

THE FORCEFUL FLOW OF HIS LIFE

Jesus, once He makes His home in you, is not sitting still, occupying only one location. We evangelicals have a phrase we use over and over: "Jesus lives in my heart." Does this phrase indoctrinate us with the idea that Jesus sits quietly in one little room and waits for you to notice Him? I'm afraid that is so. But Jesus does not sit passively in a place called "your heart." He flows through you like blood flows through your body. He runs through you like a river of Living Water, rearranging your inner landscape.

His eternal life is always working in you, when you are consciously aware of it and when you are not; when you are awake and when you are asleep. The blood is always working. Andrew Murray says in his book *The Blood of the Cross:*

We think of the shedding of the blood as an event that occurred nineteen hundred years ago on which we are to look back and, by the exercise of faith, to represent it as present and real. But as our faith is always weak, we feel that we cannot do this as it ought to be done. As a result of this mistaken idea, we have no powerful experience of what the blood can do.

The weakness of faith arises, in the case of honest hearts, from imperfect conceptions concerning the power of the blood. If I regard the blood, not

as something which lies inactive and must be aroused to activity by my faith, but as an almighty, eternal power which is always active, then my faith becomes for the first time a true faith. Then I shall understand that my weakness cannot interfere with the power of the blood . . . The blood will manifest its power in me, because the eternal Spirit of God always works with it and in it . . . .

Even once we recognize that the blood is omnipotent in its effects, we often limit the continuance of its activities to the period of our active cooperation with it. You imagine that, as long as you can think about it, and your faith is actively engaged with it, the blood will manifest its power in you. But there is a very large part of your life during which you must be engaged with earthly business, and you do not believe that, during these hours, the blood can continue its active work quite undisturbed. And yet it is so. If you have the necessary faith, if you definitely commit yourself to the sanctifying power of the blood for those hours during which you cannot be thinking about it, then you can be sure that your soul may continue, undisturbed, under the blessed activities of the blood. That is the meaning, the comfort, of what we said about the word "eternal" and the "eternal redemption" which the blood has purchased . . . .

Just as a fountain which is supplied by or from an abundant store of water streams out day and night with a cleansing and refreshing flow, so the blessed streams of this fountain of life will flow over and through the soul that dares to expect it from his Lord.

Dear friend, do you see? It's all about Him! It's not about you—how good you are, how well you have behaved, how pure your motives. It's all about Him. It's all about the streaming blood through which all the power of God flows. Your weakness is the opportunity for His power to be put on display. Just let the blood flow!

For years I have heard that the secret to peace and confidence is learning "who I am in Christ." May I be very honest with you? It never worked for me. I knew and understood that God says I am righteous, but I knew I was not righteous. I have a stubbornly logical mind, and no amount of repeating it and willing myself to accept it could make it real for me. I believed it, but it did not become real in my experience. Until . . .

Until it occurred to me: the secret is not who I am in Christ. The key to it all is *who Christ is in me*! He is Righteousness . . . in me. He is the Beloved . . . in me. He is the Victor . . . in me. It's not about who I am; it's about who He is. "Therefore I will boast all the more gladly about my weaknesses, so that Christ's power may rest on me" (2 Corinthians 12:9–10).

Are you struggling to be righteous *for* Him? Stop! Let Him be righteous *in* you. Spend time resting in who He is in you. Your only assignment is to lean on Him.

HIS ETERNAL LIFE: MY CONFIDENCE BEFORE GOD

Jesus is the one who was, who is, and who is to come. We understand trusting the Jesus who was. He came to earth and died on the cross for my sins. We understand trusting the Jesus who is to come. He will come again to set up His kingdom on earth and I will live forever with Him. But we hardly dare trust the Jesus who is. The Jesus who lives in me right now. The Jesus who lives His present-tense life through me.

Here is the startling truth. The Jesus *who was*, and the Jesus *who is to come*, is the same Jesus *who is*. It makes me want to jump up and dance!

*"God has given us eternal life, and this life is in his Son. He who has the Son has life; he who does not have the Son of God does not have life. I write these things to you who believe in the name of the Son of God so that you may know that you have eternal life. **This is the confidence we have in approaching God**: that if we ask anything according to his will, he hears us. And if we know that he hears us—whatever we ask—we know that we have what we asked of him."*
—1 John 5:11–15

In these few sentences, the Holy Spirit gives us the whole picture. My confidence before God comes from who Jesus is in me.

"God has given us eternal life . . ." God has given us a new kind of life, Jesus-life operating in an earth-body. This new life is called eternal life. It is always new, always progressing, always becoming stronger.

". . . and this life is in his Son . . ." The life God has put into us is found in only one place: in Jesus. Eternal life is Jesus' very own life that God has transfused into us.

"He who has the Son has life . . ." Jesus' life is actively flowing through us like blood is actively flowing through our bodies.

". . . he who does not have the Son does not have life." Eternal life flows only through the Son. Only those who have the Son have eternal life. Everyone else has "not life"—death—flowing in their spirit veins.

"I write these things to you who believe in the name of the Son of God so that you may know that you have eternal life." These truths are written down so that you and I can be confident that the Son's life flows through us; so that we can believe in the present-tense life of Jesus operating in us. When the Father looks at me, He does not see "Jennifer, who believes in Jesus." He sees "Jesus in His Jennifer form." This is called eternal life!

"This is the confidence we have in approaching God: that if we ask anything according to his will, he hears us. And if we know that he hears us—whatever we ask—we know that we have what we asked of him." When the life of Jesus is operating in me at full power, I can know the will of God and pray with confidence.

HIS LIFE IN ME CREATES MY DESIRES

The Son, whose will is perfectly at one with the Father's will, is living in me. He is continually washing away flesh (Adam-life) and replacing it with Spirit (Jesus-life). I can trust Him to use my mind, my imagination, my desires, my understanding and intellect as conduits through which to express the will of God.

▼

"If you remain in me and my words remain in you, ask whatever you wish, and it will be given you. This is to my Father's glory, that you bear much fruit, showing yourselves to be my disciples." —John 15:7–8

Using these words from Scripture as your guide, answer the following questions.

1. Write out the "if-then" statement (the "then" is implied):

If_____

Then _____

2. In an "if-then" statement, the "if" clause *causes* the "then" clause. Explain the relationship between the "if" and the "then" in this statement.

3. *If* you soak yourself in His Word and let it live in you, *then* you will experience answers to prayer. Is that what you saw? His Word actively works in you to create His desires. *"It is God who works in you to will . . . his good purpose"* (Philippians 2:13). The next sentence in John 15:8 builds on that understanding: *"This is to my Father's glory."* What is to His Father's glory? Go back to the sentence upon which He is building.

4. What is to His Father's glory? Answered prayer! Why? What does answered prayer do? Look at the next phrase: *"that you bear much fruit, showing yourself to be my disciples."* Fruit always means an outer result of an inner work. What is the fruit He has been talking about here?

5. The fruit here is answered prayer. How will answered prayer prove that you are Jesus' disciple?

▲

His life flowing through me creates desires that match His. If His blood is flowing freely, He is molding and shaping my prayers.

"This is to my Father's glory . . . ." What is to His Father's glory? Answered prayer! Answered prayer is the fruit of the Vine's life through the branch. It is the authenticating mark of the present-tense life of Christ in me. The fruit on a branch identifies what kind of vine it is. You know a tree by its fruit. The life of Christ flowing through you creates the desires of Christ in you, which produces the will of Christ through you in the form of answered prayer.

This is your confidence before God—the confidence that whatever you ask of Him, He hears you, and gives you what you have asked of Him—the eternal life of Christ in you.

Oh, the love that drew salvation's plan!
Oh, the grace that brought it down to man!
Oh, the mighty gulf that God did span
At Calvary.

—"At Calvary" by William R. Newell

REFLECT

"Let us fix our eyes on Jesus, the author and perfecter of our faith." —Hebrews 12:2

Spend time right now simply dwelling on Jesus. Behold Him with the eyes of your heart. Let your inner eyes be blinded to everything else by the brightness of His glory. He has made you His home. He lives in you. Let the reality of His presence settle on you. Let Him relieve you of your burdens; let Him bring an end to your earnest striving to please Him. Write out your thoughts, if you wish.

Just let the blood flow!

_____

_____

_____

_____

_____

_____

THE OVERCOMING LIFE

DAY ONE

Read the following Scriptures and answer these questions.

"I have told you these things, so that in me you may have peace. In this world you will have trouble. But take heart! I have overcome the world." —John 16:33

"They overcame him by the blood of the Lamb and by the word of their testimony." —Revelation 12:11

1. How would you define the word "overcome"?

2. In John 16:33, who did the overcoming?

3. In Revelation 12:11, who does the overcoming?

4. What or who is to be overcome?

We need to understand this: What is Jesus' victory over the world (the realm of Satan's influence) and over Satan himself? How is Jesus' victory translated to us so that it is our victory?

The word *overcome* means to subdue or to win the victory over. Let's examine how Jesus overcame the world and how His overcoming life becomes my victory. Why does Jesus say that you and I can take heart, or have courage, because *He* has overcome the world? Don't I have to overcome the world myself? And how do I overcome Satan by the blood of the Lamb? How are "the blood of the Lamb" and "the word of [my] testimony" two parts of one whole? In order to understand this, we have to start with Jesus' role as the last Adam.

The first Adam was:
• The beginning point of humanity
• A new creation
• The father of a race; all humanity bears the imprint of Adam (1 Cor. 15:48)
• All of the above

The first Adam:
• Was overcome (defeated) by the pull of sin
• Was the door through which death entered the world
• Both of the above

THE LAST ADAM

In Romans 5:14, Adam is called *"a pattern of the one to come."* In 1 Corinthians 15:45, Jesus is called *"the last Adam."* Clearly Adam and Jesus are to be compared. If we are invited to this comparison, then there is obviously some new truth to be understood from it.

Read Romans 5:12–21. Read it phrase by phrase, taking time to comprehend a thought at a time. Don't feel overwhelmed by its complexities, because we will break it down and look into its message. Just familiarize yourself with the concepts.

Chart the statements about the first Adam and the last Adam.

FIRST ADAM	LAST ADAM

Romans 5:12–21 compares the two Adams, the first Adam and the last Adam. Just as sin and death entered the world through a man—the first Adam—so righteousness and life must enter the world through a man—the last Adam. By calling Jesus the last Adam, the Spirit is telling us that what one man did, the other man un-did.

In the comparison, Paul first points out their similarities in verses 12–14. Then he points to their differences in verses 15–21. This is a reasonable way to compare two things. If we were going to compare two apples, as we held them apart, we might first notice all the things that are alike: both are red on the outside and white on the inside; both have black seeds arranged in a star-pattern; both have a stem. However, when we place them side-by-side we would notice their differences: one is a different shade of red than the other; one's stem is thicker than the other's; one is bigger than the other. So it makes sense for us to follow Paul's pattern as we look at the two Adams.

"Adam" in this context is Adam and Eve as a unit. "So God created man in his own image, in the image of God he created him; male and female he created them" (Genesis 1:27). The Hebrew word *adam* means "clay or dirt." There are times in Scripture when Adam and Eve are dealt with as separate beings. And indeed they were two separate beings—one male, one female. But in this discussion, Paul is using "Adam" to mean the two as a unit—humanity. This is important to see, because in this comparison, some of the actions are specifically those of the female *adam*, Eve, rather than the male *adam*.

What was Jesus' job as the last Adam? He came to undo everything the first Adam had done. He came to bring a halt to everything Adam put in motion. He came to restore the proper order and reverse the curse. Just as the curse of death came through a man, so the restoration of the blessing must come through a man. Just as sin came through a man, so righteousness must come through a man. Just as one man brought death, so one man would bring life.

When, from the cross, Jesus said, "It is finished," He was using a word that meant that a mission had been completed or a task accomplished. The task to which He was referring was His job as the last Adam. The whole salvation work was not completed until He rose from the dead, ascended to the right hand of the Father, and came to indwell believers in Spirit-form. The story of His redeeming work did not end at the cross. His job as redeemer was completed when, from the right hand of the Father, He poured out His Spirit upon believers (Acts 2:29–36). At the moment of His physical death on the cross, He completed His job as the last Adam. Let me say it again: **The job that was finished at the cross was His job as the last Adam**.

THE TWO ADAMS

Let's see how the first Adam was a pattern of the last Adam. Let's first examine their similarities.

Both had a body specifically created by God. You know this is true for the first Adam. God created him from the dust of the earth and created her from his rib. Neither male nor female *adam* was the product of the sexual union between man and woman. Read Genesis 2:7 and Genesis 2:21–22.

This is also the case with the last Adam. We know that He was not the product of the sexual union between a man and a woman, but was created by the power of the Holy Spirit. The angel described the process by which Jesus would be formed in Mary's womb in a direct echo of the creation account. "The Holy Spirit will come upon you and the power of the Most High will overshadow you," (Luke 1:35). "The Spirit of God was hovering over the waters," (Genesis 1:2). The Holy Spirit hovering and overshadowing was the active force carrying out the Word of Creation.

Both the first Adam and the last Adam had a human soul (mind, will, and emotions) through which temptation could come. Therefore, both had the openings through which sin can enter. In Hebrews 4:15 we read of Jesus that He has been *"tempted in every way, just as we are—yet was without sin."* He was tempted just as we are—by the same methods, through the same channels.

There is a debate among theologians about whether or not it was possible for Jesus to have sinned, since He was God. The debate is not whether He *did* sin. Both sides agree that He did not. Rather, the debate is whether it was *possible* for Him to sin. The theological term is "Christ's impeccability." One side of the debate holds that He could not have sinned because He was God. The other side of the debate says that if it were not really possible for Him to have sinned, then He was never really tempted. Whichever side of that debate you identify with, I ask you to keep an open mind until you have gone through this week's material and next week's material. Let me assure you that I do not believe that Jesus ever, for even one second, entertained an evil desire or had a sinful inclination. Yet I do think that the Scripture shows us that His temptation was very real.

Jesus, when He lived in the body of a man, did not just have the physical arrangement of body parts so that He resembled a man, or passed for a man. He became a man. He took upon Himself the complete form of a man. He lived His Spirit-life through a human soul, in an earth body. You'll see this in more detail in next week's material. **The first Adam was tempted at each level of his humanity—body, soul, and spirit.**

Read Genesis 3:1–6. What three things did Eve, the female *adam*, see about the fruit of the forbidden tree?

---

*"When the woman saw that the fruit of the tree was **good for food** and **pleasing to the eye**, and also **desirable for gaining wisdom**, she took and ate it"* (Genesis 3:6).

She saw that it was good for food: an appeal to her body.

She saw that it was pleasing to the eye: an appeal to her soul.

She saw that it was desirable for gaining wisdom: an appeal to her spirit.

The tempter had said that if she were wise she would be *"like God, knowing good and evil"* (Genesis 3:5). This was the same desire that had been Lucifer's downfall: *"I will make myself like the Most High"* (Isaiah 14:14). This third attraction, then, was an appeal to her spiritual nature, by which she knew to worship and obey only God.

The forbidden tree was the Tree of the Knowledge of Good and Evil. You might think, "Wouldn't it make more sense to say that the fruit of the tree would cause them to know evil? After all, they already knew good." Did they know good? Some things you can only know by their opposites. You can only know light if you know dark. You can only know up if you know down. Unless they knew evil, they would not know good. They just knew what was. They did not know it as "good" until they came to know evil. So even though the fruit of the only tree forbidden her appealed to perfectly legitimate desires—the desire for food and the delight in beauty—it ultimately led to spiritual downfall. Her good desires were the openings through which temptation entered and brought sin.

Notice something interesting: Eve saw that the fruit was *"good for food and pleasing to the eye, and also desirable for gaining wisdom."* Here is how the Scripture describes all the trees that God made for *adam* to enjoy: *"Now the LORD God had planted a garden in the east, in Eden; and there he put the man he had formed. And the LORD God made all kinds of trees grow out of the ground—trees that were **pleasing to the eye** and **good for food**"* (Genesis 2:8–9). Do you see the echo of the phrases?

The deceiver appealed to her legitimate desires (a delight to the eyes) and played on her God-given needs (good for food) to lead her to believe that she could find a way to satisfy those needs and desires on her own (desirable for gaining wisdom). She could be wise herself instead of looking to Wisdom Himself (1 Corinthians 1:24, 30). *She could be her own source.* Keep this in mind as we move through this week and next week. Ultimately the temptation to which the first Adam fell was this: You can be your own source. You can do for yourself that which God has promised to do for you. You can obtain for yourself that which God has promised to give you. You can be like God.

The last Adam was tempted at each level of his humanity—body, soul, and spirit.

▼

Read Matthew 4:3–11. Write down the three temptations.

The last Adam, Jesus, in His earth-body, had the same openings the first Adam had. He had a human soul (mind, will, and emotions). He had a human body. Satan's most direct assault on Him, in the desert following His baptism, took the same path as the tempter's assault on the first Adam. Each level of His humanity was tested—body, soul, and spirit. Satan was looking for an opening. The encounter is recorded in Matthew 4:3–11.

1. Tell these stones to become bread—an appeal to His body.

2. Throw Yourself off the highest point of the temple and let the angels rescue you in the sight of everyone. Prove Yourself to them the easy way—an appeal to His soul. It made a certain kind of sense and was an appeal to His mind. "What a good way to gather the people to Myself!" It was an appeal to His emotions. He could save both Himself and the people He loved great pain by short-circuiting the process. It appealed to His will. He desired for the people He came to save to see the truth and turn to Him.

3. I will give you all the kingdoms of the world if you will just bow down and worship me—an appeal to His spirit. It is His destiny that He will possess all the kingdoms of the world. All He had to do was worship one other than the Father and that which was rightfully His would be in His possession now.

In each case, the tempter appealed to Jesus' legitimate and right desires and needs. Each thing that the enemy dangled before Jesus was in line with God's desires for Him.

• God desired to meet Jesus' physical needs. He lived in a body that required food and it was God's desire that Jesus' body would be nourished.

• God desired that people would recognize Jesus as the Messiah and would come to Him.

• It was God's desire—had always been the plan—that Jesus would rule over the kingdoms of the world.

The tempter wanted to convince Jesus to use His own resources to get His needs met. He wanted Jesus to take over and "do God's will" in His own power. He wanted Jesus to be His own source.

FIRST ADAM	LAST ADAM
God created earth-body; (Genesis 2:7)	God created earth-body; (Luke 1:35)
Begins life without the taint of sin	Begins life without the taint of sin
Has human soul (mind, will, emotions) and can be tempted	Has human soul (mind, will, emotions) and can be tempted
Was tempted at each level of his humanity	Was tempted at each level of His humanity

THE TWO ADAMS

Read Genesis 3:1–24. Focus for a minute on verse 6. Had the woman ever seen the forbidden tree before?

She knew where it was located. She knew exactly which tree it was, among all the trees. Do you reach the conclusion that she had looked at the tree many times before?

In verse 6, what is different this time?

Does it seem to you that this is the first time she has been tempted?

Did either she or the male *adam* expend any effort to resist temptation?

Now, look at the passage again. I want you to read these verses and assign each a heading or a topic. I want you to see at a glance the progression of events. I'll do the first one so you can see what I want you to do.

Verses	Heading
Verses 1–5	"Adam and Eve are tempted"
Verse 6	
Verses 7–13	
Verses 14–20	
Verses 21–24	

Next, let's examine how the last Adam reversed everything the first Adam did. The first Adam was man made in the image of God (Genesis 1:26). The last Adam was God made in the image of man (Philippians 2:7–8).

The first Adam responded immediately to temptation. The account suggests no resistance on the part of the first Adam. It seems to assume that this is the first time Adam or Eve had been confronted with temptation. Apparently the appeal of the forbidden tree had not occurred to them before. The account says that when ("as soon as") Eve saw that the tree was good for food, a delight to the eyes, and to be desired to make men wise, immediately she yielded.

Consider that when God told Adam and Eve that when ("as soon as") they ate from the forbidden tree they would surely (without question, definitely) die, they had no experiential knowledge of what death was. Death had never occurred in their experience. They had no concrete concept of death.

The first death on the earth occurred when, to cover their sinful state, God killed an animal and used its skin as a covering for *adam*, both male and female. So when you think about this account, do not imagine that they had a clear idea of the "death" they were admitting into their experience. This is one of the reasons that they fell so easily into sin. They did not know what death was.

The last Adam resisted temptation even to the point of shedding blood. *"For we do not have a high priest who is unable to sympathize with our weaknesses, but we have one who has been tempted in every way, just as we are—yet was without sin"* (Hebrews 4:15–16). *"Consider him who endured such opposition from sinful men, so that you will not grow weary and lose heart. In your struggle against sin, you have not yet resisted to the point of shedding your blood"* (Hebrews 12:3–4). The last Adam was tempted in every way, yet resisted to the very end. When He was shedding His blood on the cross, He was resisting temptation. Satan was tempting Him to the very last, tempting Him to take Himself out of the Father's hands and be His own source.

The first Adam was covered. His sin was the cause of the first death: the death of the animal whose skins were used for their covering. When the first Adam sinned, God provided both female *adam* and male *adam* with a covering that required the shedding of blood. They had immediately covered themselves with leaves, but that covering was inadequate. They had to be covered by nothing but blood. It cost a life to make an adequate covering for the first Adam.

Before their sin introduced the need for a blood covering, the first Adam had lived in harmony with the animals. There was perfectly peaceful co-existence. The animals in the garden were to them, I imagine, like beloved pets. He had even named them himself. When the first sin cost the death of an animal, Adam and Eve were not emotionally distanced from that act. They were, I'm sure, horrified to learn what death was and that it would be inflicted on an innocent animal on their behalf. In a very real and graphic way, another paid the price for their sin.

The last Adam was uncovered. In the crucifixion account, He is progressively stripped of His clothing until He hung naked and exposed on the cross. *"When the soldiers crucified Jesus, they took his clothes, dividing them into four shares, one for each of them, with the undergarment remaining"* (John 19:23).

As He hung naked on the cross, He was covered by nothing except His own blood. As His blood streamed from His veins, it poured over Him and covered His body, where He bore our sins. *"He himself bore our sins in his body on the tree"* (1 Peter 2:24). His own blood covered Him, and in Him, covered our sins. He who knew no sin became sin for us. Our sin cost His life. He paid the price.

For the first Adam, the Tree of Life became a "tree of death" to him. He was protected from it. Remember that there were two trees in the midst of the garden, one forbidden (Tree of the Knowledge of Good and Evil), one not forbidden (Tree of Life).

"Now the LORD God had planted a garden in the east, in Eden; and there he put the man he had formed. And the LORD God made all kinds of trees grow out of the ground—trees that were pleasing to the eye and good for food. In the middle of the garden were the tree of life and the tree of the knowledge of good and evil."
—Genesis 2:8–9

"And the LORD God commanded the man, 'You are free to eat from any tree in the garden; but you must not eat from the tree of the knowledge of good and evil, for when you eat of it you will surely die.'" —Genesis 2:16–17

Sin was introduced when Adam and Eve ate from the forbidden tree. Sin brings death; sin and death are two sides of one coin. The moment sin entered the experience of mankind, death accompanied it. At the instant Adam and Eve bit into the fruit from the forbidden tree, death entered their spirits. "Not life" began to flow through their spirit-veins. Their physical bodies, designed to be containers of life, became containers of death. Their problem was not simply the absence of life, but the presence of death.

The death that had entered them would be manifested in their life experience. God described for them the curse that sin-death had brought into their lives in Genesis 3:14–19. He described how death would be lived out.

After He had fully pronounced the curse and punishment, Elohim (the Three-One; Father, Son, and Spirit) said, *"The man* (both male and female *adam) has now become like one of us, knowing good and evil. He must not be allowed to reach out his hand and take also from the tree of life and eat, and live forever"* (Genesis 3:22, parentheses added).

Look carefully. This is separate from the punishment phase. Did you notice that when you outlined the passage? God is saying that mankind might still live forever, even though death had now entered their experience. He is saying that Adam and Eve must not be allowed to eat from the Tree of Life or else they will live forever. They were already dead, yet they might live forever.

Clearly, the fruit of the Tree of Life maintained the physical body and prolonged physical life. Since mankind's body had now become a container of death, if his body lasted forever, he would be doomed to live forever in a state of death. In order to protect Adam and Eve and all of their descendants from living forever in a state of death, Elohim set a guard to keep them from prolonging their living death, or their "hell on earth." The dilemma was this: Though he were dead (spiritually), yet shall he live (physically).

"And the LORD God said, 'The man has now become like one of us, knowing good and evil. He must not be allowed to reach out his had and take also from the tree of life and eat, and live forever.' So the LORD God banished him from the Garden of Eden to work the ground from which he had been taken. After he drove the man out, he placed on the east side of the Garden of Eden cherubim and a flaming sword flashing back and forth to guard the way to the tree of life."
—Genesis 3:22–24

Do you see? The Tree of Life had become a "tree of death" to Adam and he was protected from it. The first Adam was driven from the Garden of Eden and barred from the Tree of Life as protection, not punishment.

For the last Adam, the "tree of death"—the cross—became the Tree of Life for mankind. *"He himself bore our sins in his body on the tree, so that we might die to sins and live for righteousness; by his wounds you have been healed"* (1 Peter 2:24). A tree is recognized by its fruit (Genesis 1:12; Luke 6:44). What is the fruit that hung on the tree of death, the cross? The eternal life! The cross became the Tree of Life.

Jesus poured out His blood so that we might die to sin—be eternally declared separated from our sins. Then, when "this body of sin has been done away with," we can live for righteousness. By His wounds, we are made whole. We now partake of His life (2 Peter 1:4)—eat from the Tree of Life. His "tree of death" became our Tree of Life. Now He reverses the dilemma that the first Adam brought. Jesus says, *"Though he were dead (physically), yet shall he live (spiritually)"* (John 11:25 KJV, parentheses mine).

While the first Adam tasted sin and brought death, the last Adam tasted death and brought life. While the first Adam was protected from the Tree of Life, the last Adam was led to the "tree of death." While the first Adam was kept from the Tree of Life, the last Adam was handed over by God (Acts 2:23) to *"taste death for everyone"* (Hebrews 2:9) by hanging on the tree.

The first Adam's bride was taken from his side without the shedding of blood. *"So the LORD God caused the man to fall into a deep sleep; and while he was sleeping, he took one of the man's ribs and closed up the place with flesh. Then the LORD God made a woman from the rib he had taken out of the man, and he brought her to the man"* (Genesis 2:21–22). The first Adam greeted his bride by calling her *"bone of my bones and flesh of my flesh"* and they became one flesh (Genesis 2:23–24).

The last Adam also had His side opened and from it flowed water and blood—Spirit and life. His bride, the church, is born of His Spirit and His blood. As the first Adam and his bride became one flesh, the last Adam and His bride become one Spirit. *"He who unites himself with the Lord is one with him in spirit"* (1 Corinthians 6:17). Do you suppose that Jesus says of us, "Here at last is spirit of My Spirit and blood of My blood"?

REVERSAL: First Adam	REVERSAL: Last Adam
Gave in without a fight (Genesis 3:6)	Fought to the end and never gave in (Hebrews 12:4; 4:15)
Covered (Genesis 3:21)	Uncovered (John 19:23)
Tree of Life became a "tree of death" to him; he was protected from it (Genesis 3:22–24)	"Tree of death" (cross) became a Tree of Life to us; He was led to it (Romans 6:3–5)
Tasted sin and brought death (Genesis 2:17)	"Tasted death" and brought life (Hebrews 2:9)
Bride created from bone taken out of his side without shedding of blood (Genesis 2:21–22)	Bride is new creation from "the water and the blood" that came out of His side by the shedding of blood (John 19:34)

Jesus' job as the last Adam was to reverse, step by step, everything the first Adam did. He had to face the same challenges that confronted the first Adam, but to resist sin where the first Adam fell into sin. He regained what Adam lost.

DAY THREE

As we continue to examine His job as the last Adam, we will come to understand why Jesus had to live out His Spirit-life in an earth-body in order to *become* our salvation. We are saved by His life, but His life did not become available to us—did not flow through us—until He had finished the work God gave Him to do.

Get ready. We are about to put some pieces together that will lead you to a conclusion about the precious blood of the Lamb that will make you fall on your face in the presence of such overwhelming love. You will never be the same once you have seen this.

The first Adam had corrupted flesh by giving it supremacy over his spirit. Here is an illustration of the structure of mankind, from the first Adam until the present.

The design for man was that spirit would rule soul, and soul would rule body. He was to be a being whose life and power originated in his spirit. Instead, the first Adam let his body and soul—his flesh—rule over his spirit. He became a being ruled by his flesh. As the last Adam, God assigned Jesus to purify and perfect flesh, by keeping it subject to Spirit.

▼

Remembering yesterday's material, what was the underlying temptation that defined every one of Jesus' temptations?

Look at the following Scriptures to identify the underlying power that defined Jesus' activities.

"For the one whom God has sent speaks the words of God, for God gives the Spirit without limit. The Father loves the Son and has placed everything in his hands." —John 3:34–35

"Jesus gave them this answer: 'I tell you the truth, the Son can do nothing by himself; he can do only what he sees his Father doing, because whatever the Father does the Son also does. For the Father loves the Son and shows him all he does.'" —John 5:19–20

"For the very work that the Father has given me to finish, and which I am doing, testifies that the Father has sent me." —John 5:36

"Just as the living Father sent me and I live because of the Father, so the one who feeds on me will live because of me." —John 6:57

"But if I do judge, my decisions are right, because I am not alone. I stand with the Father, who sent me." —John 8:16

"I do nothing on my own but speak just what the Father has taught me. The one who sent me is with me; he has not left me alone, for I always do what pleases him." —John 8:28–29

"Jesus replied, 'If I glorify myself, my glory means nothing. My Father, whom you claim as your God, is the one who glorifies me.'" —John 8:54

"The reason my Father loves me is that I lay down my life—only to take it up again. No one takes it from me, but I lay it down of my own accord. I have authority to lay it down and authority to take it up again. This command I received from my Father." —John 10:17–18

"For I did not speak of my own accord, but the Father who sent me commanded me what to say and how to say it. I know that his command leads to eternal life. So whatever I say is just what the Father has told me to say." —John 12:49–50

"The words I say to you are not just my own. Rather, it is the Father, living in me, who is doing his work." —John 14:10

"These words you hear are not my own; they belong to the Father who sent me." —John 14:24

"The world must learn that I love the Father and that I do exactly what my Father has commanded me." —John 14:31

Who was Jesus' source?

Jesus did not use His own power, but relied on the power of the Father working through Him. This was the key to everything. His soul was surrendered to be the servant of the Father. His soul was the vehicle through which the Father did the Father's work. This is the dynamic that the enemy was working continually to disrupt.

JESUS WORKED OUT OUR SALVATION

The process of our salvation, which Jesus fully accomplished, did not begin at His death on the cross. It began the very moment He was conceived in the womb of Mary. If the only thing necessary to save me were His death on the cross, He could have arrived on earth as a full-grown man just in time to die on the cross. The Book of Hebrews tells us that Jesus *"became the source of eternal salvation for all who obey him"* (Hebrews 5:9). It speaks of an unfolding purpose being worked out over a period of time. That whole sentence says, *"Although he was a son, he learned obedience from what he suffered and, **once made perfect**, he became the source of eternal salvation to all who obey him"* (Hebrews 5:8–9). In tomorrow's material, we will wade right into the depths of this verse, but right now I want you to see that Jesus was being perfected. A process was being worked out.

To *perfect* means to bring to final form. The Scripture is not suggesting that Jesus was flawed or had sins to overcome. It is saying that He had to be completed, finalized, finished. When could He say "It is finished"? On the cross.

The Greek word translated "finished" in John 19:30 is *teleo*, which means to complete, to fulfill, to discharge a duty. The Greek word translated "perfect" in Hebrews 5:9 is *teleioo*, which means to accomplish, finish, bring to a proposed end, to reach a goal, to add what is lacking in order to render a thing full. Do you see how closely related the two words are? Both are from the same root word.

Jesus' spirit was already fully formed, perfect, finished. It was His man-soul that was being brought to completion. Jesus started out as a human with an *innocent and sinless* soul, but only through testing could His soul become *perfect*. From first to last, during His 33 years in the body and soul of a man, He was perfecting the soul. In order to carry out that assignment, the last Adam had to live in flesh.

▼

Read this description of Jesus found in Philippians 2:6–7 from the New American Standard Bible:

"Who, although He existed in the form of God, did not regard equality with God a thing to be grasped, but emptied Himself, taking the form of a bond-servant, and being made in the likeness of men. Being found in appearance as a man, He humbled Himself by becoming obedient to the point of death, even death on a cross."

1. What was the eternal essence and nature of Jesus?

2. Before He became flesh, He was "equal" with God the Father. What does that equality imply? i.e., In what ways were the Father and the Son equal?

3. When He took on flesh and was born of woman, the Son gave up this particular equality with God. This passage tells us that although He was equal with God in power and authority, He did not consider that equality something of which He could not let go. Instead of holding that equality in a tight-fisted grasp, He *let it go*. He emptied Himself. Of what did He empty Himself? (Consider His dependence upon the Father, His obedience to the Father, etc.)

4. Although He laid aside His power and authority as God in order to let the Father work through Him, did He ever lay aside His nature as God? Was He always of one essence with the Father? (Consider John 12:44–45; 14:7; and 10:30.)

He took "the form of a bond-servant." To whom was He subservient? Although He served and met the needs of man, whom was He obeying? Whose bond-servant did He willingly become?

He took on "the likeness of man." He took on the structure of a man—body and soul. He lived His Spirit-life through the body and the soul of a man. In taking on the form of man, do you see that He took on the limitations and the needs of humanity?

▲

Philippians 2:6–7 tells us that Jesus took on the nature of a man. He took on a nature that could be tempted. He temporarily emptied Himself of that aspect of His God-nature that cannot be tempted. He had to be tempted in order to overcome (wrestle to the ground, triumph over) sin. By putting Himself in enemy territory—going behind the lines—Jesus was exposing Himself to sin's power. His soul was continually being put to the test. Where the first Adam failed, the last Adam triumphed. **Through the process of His earth-life, He was developing an antidote to sin and death.**

DAY FOUR

JESUS' BLOOD: OUR SALVATION

Jesus overcame the power of sin by direct exposure to its poison. The earth-picture of this spirit-truth is our body's ability to produce immunity. Our physical blood is the battleground between the immune system and invaders such as viruses or bacteria. When illness invades your body, your blood produces antibodies specifically designed to defeat that exact invader. Once your blood has built up enough antibodies against a specific disease, that disease will never have the opportunity to develop in your bloodstream. When you are exposed to that disease, it will be met with an army of destroyers already in place. You are immune. It may invade your body again, but it is defeated before it even makes an appearance. You have overcome that disease. The overcoming power is in your blood.

Immunity works by employing the blood's ability to build up antibodies against a specific invader, rendering that invader powerless in future encounters. Should the disease ever show up again, immunity is already in place. The germ has no time to procreate and invade the body before it is destroyed by the antibodies. You might say that your body is "dead" (unresponsive) to that disease.

In the spiritual realm, the disease that invades our lives is called sin. God wants to defeat sin in each individual life.

God Himself is never exposed to sin. He cannot be tempted by sin (James 1:13). In other words, the life of God cannot develop an immunity to sin because the sin disease has no access to Him. That's why He came in the form of man, in the shape of flesh. So that He could place Himself within the reach of sin, combat it head-on, develop a spiritual immune system that could be passed on to all who would be born again and accept His life as their own. He has overcome the sin disease and longs to transfuse you with His sin-immune life.

JESUS' SPIRITUAL IMMUNITIES

God used temptation as a training ground for His Son. Jesus had to face and overcome temptation so that He could be the victor. His life had to develop immunity to sin by exposure to the sin-germ so that He could pass along to those who obey Him eternal salvation (freedom from the evil one). The life that flows through you and me—His saving life—has already conquered sin. Andrew Murray, in his book *The Holiest of All,* puts it this way:

As Adam never could have brought us under the power of sin and death, if he had not been our father, communicating to us his own nature, so Christ never could save us, except by taking our nature upon Him, doing in that nature all that we would need to do, had it been possible for us to deliver ourselves, and then communicating the fruit of what He effected as a nature within us to be the power of a new, an eternal life. As a divine necessity, without which there could be no salvation, as an act of infinite love and condescension, the Son of God became a partaker of flesh and blood. So alone could He be the Second Adam, the Father of a new race.

Read 2 Corinthians 5:21: *"God made him who had no sin to be sin for us, so that in him we might become the righteousness of God."*

In light of your study so far, what do you perceive this verse to be conveying?

Read Romans 6:10–11: *"The death he died, he died to sin once for all; but the life he lives, he lives to God. In the same way, count yourselves dead to sin but alive to God in Christ Jesus."*

In light of your study so far, what do you perceive this verse to be conveying?

Surely He took up our infirmities and carried our sorrows. He withstood the punishing onslaught of the evil one in order to bring us peace. He fought and won the battles that would have doomed us to death so we would not have to fight them. We can stand still and see the salvation of the Lord. My friend, do you see? Every time Jesus faced the enemy, it was for you. Every temptation Jesus endured and triumphed over was for you. Victory by victory, the antibodies against sin were being formed. Encounter by encounter, your salvation was being worked out in the blood of Jesus.

DAY FIVE

What was the process the Father used to develop spiritual antibodies in Jesus?

Jesus had no unrighteousness because He never let unrighteousness take root. He never once sinned because He had no unrighteousness that led Him to sin. But as a human, He had the human needs and instincts through which unrighteousness can enter. This is why He could be tempted, unlike the Father, who cannot be tempted. How did God use temptation to accomplish His purpose for Jesus?

"In bringing many sons to glory, it was fitting that God . . . should make the author of their salvation perfect through suffering" (Hebrews 2:10). God made Jesus perfect through suffering. *Perfect* means the bringing of a thing to that completeness of condition designed for it. The writer of Hebrews is not saying that Jesus used to be sinful, then became sinless. He is saying that the man Jesus, the earth-man, grew and matured into His role as author of salvation for all who believe. God accomplished this maturing process through suffering.

"Although he was a son, he learned obedience from what he suffered and, once made perfect, he became the source of eternal salvation for all who obey him" (Hebrews 5:8). Again, Jesus *learned* obedience. He was never disobedient, but He continually progressed to deeper levels of obedience as deeper levels were required. He progressed to the point where He could be *"obedient to death—even death on a cross"* (Philippians 2:8). The Father did not require the same level of obedience from 12-year-old Jesus as He did from 20-year-old Jesus. Nor did He require the same level of obedience from 20-year-old Jesus as He did from 33-year-old Jesus. God trained His Son step by step. He trained Him in deeper levels of obedience through what He suffered.

Two times, then, we read that Jesus was matured through suffering. What kind of suffering did God use to mature Jesus? What did Jesus suffer that brought Him to that completeness of condition designed for Him? This is not referring to the suffering of the cross. This suffering had to produce maturity before He could go to the cross. Through suffering, He *became* the source of eternal salvation.

Read Hebrews 2:18— *"Because he himself suffered when he was tempted, he is able to help those who are being tempted."*

　　　　When did Jesus suffer?

What kind of suffering, then, matured Jesus?

How did the enemy's battle plan become the very process by which he was defeated?

---------------------------▲---------------------------

We find the description of His suffering in this passage. *"Because he himself suffered when he was tempted, he is able to help those who are being tempted"* (Hebrews 2:18). He suffered when He was tempted. The suffering through which the Father trained the Son in obedience: temptation. The suffering by which the last Adam completed His task: temptation. The suffering that perfected the man-soul of Jesus: temptation.

God's visit to our planet is primarily remembered not for its display of raw power but for its example of representative suffering. A pattern emerges through the refining fire of suffering: God responds to evil not by obliterating it, but by making evil itself serve a higher good. He overcame evil by absorbing it, taking it on Himself, and, finally, by forgiving it. Jesus overcame as the One who goes before, by going right through the center of temptation, evil, and death.
—From *In His Image,* by Philip Yancey and Paul Brand

Look more closely at this passage in Hebrews. *"During the days of Jesus' life on earth, he offered up prayers and petitions with loud cries and tears to the one who could save him from death, and he was heard because of his reverent submission. Although he was a son, he learned obedience from what he suffered and, once made perfect, he became the source of eternal salvation for all who obey him"* (Hebrews 5:7–9).

During Jesus' earth-life, He prayed with passion (*"loud cries and tears"*) to the One who could save Him from death. Does this refer to death on the cross? No. This sentence is talking about a habit of Jesus', not a one-time occurrence. During, or throughout, His days on earth, He repeatedly offered up prayers and petitions. This entire passage is describing the process of Jesus' training. By calling the Father "the one who could save him from death," the writer is giving us a hint about the content of these impassioned outpourings of prayer. Jesus is calling out to be saved from death—and God heard and answered Him. The Greek word for "heard" means to respond. In other words, the Scripture says that Jesus asked to be saved from death and the Father saved Him from death. What kind of death? The death that is part of the sin package. Jesus was crying out to be rescued from the sin that would bring His mission to failure and leave us in our death state. This intense suffering, struggling against sin, taught Him deep obedience and forged Him into the author of eternal salvation.

"Since the children have flesh and blood, he too shared in their humanity so that by his death he might destroy him who holds the power of death—that is, the devil—and free those who all their lives were held in slavery by their fear of death. For surely it is not angels he helps, but Abraham's descendants. For this reason he had to be made like his brothers in every way, in order that he might become a merciful and faithful high priest in service to God, and that he might make atonement for the sins of the people. Because he himself suffered when he was tempted, he is able to help those who are being tempted."
—Hebrews 2:14–18

Jesus became a partaker of our nature (Hebrews 2:14) so that we could become a partaker of His nature (2 Peter 1:4). When we read that He is able to help those who are being tempted because He Himself was tempted, we begin to understand how we overcome by the blood of the Lamb. It is not saying that now Jesus knows how it feels to be tempted, so He can cheer us on when we are tempted. It is saying that Jesus overcame sin and won the victory over temptation, creating the "antibodies" in His blood. He has transfused His blood into our spirit-veins. Therefore, when we are facing temptation, we need only yield to His life and His power running through us. The word *help* has the sense of "rescue" or "relieve." He has already overcome sin, and the antibodies are in His blood. Don't fight harder against the temptation; instead yield more fully to His life. Turn inward where the victory runs through your soul.

He inflicted a deadly wound on sin, gaining the victory in his own person . . . If the Lord Jesus was to become our true Saviour one thing was most necessary—He must deliver us from ourselves . . . And there is no other means by which this can be prepared for us, except by the Lord Jesus opening the path for us, obtaining a new life for us, and imparting it to us.
—From *The Blood of the Cross*, by Andrew Murray

The One who knew no sin became sin for us. (Note that He did not become *sinful* for us.) He allowed His pure, unblemished soul to be exposed to the sin-germ for our sakes. He became sin *for us* so that He could be righteousness *in us*. What a Savior!

Jesus Christ did not convey Himself genetically. If He had, his offspring would have been one-half Christ, one-fourth Christ, one-sixteenth Christ, on through His distant descendants of modern times when faint evidence of His bloodline would remain. Rather, He chose to convey Himself personally and nutritiously, offering to each one of us the power of His own resurrected life. No other New Testament image, . . . expresses the concept of "Christ in you" so well as does blood.
—From *In His Image,* by Philip Yancey and Paul Brand

THE OVERCOMING LIFE

"I have told you these things, so that in me you may have peace. In this world you will have trouble. But take heart! I have overcome the world." —John 16:33

"They overcame him by the blood of the Lamb and by the word of their testimony" —Revelation 12:11

We overcome the evil one by the blood of the Lamb running through our spirit-veins. We overcome sin and the world's influence by the power of His life. It is not faith in the blood that overcomes the enemy, but the blood itself. This is the word of my testimony: Christ in me, the hope of glory!

REFLECT

Let the eyes of your heart gaze upon your Tree of Life. See the blood streaming from His wounds to cover you. Let it settle deep in your heart that His overcoming life flows from His veins through you.

Oh, that old rugged cross,
So despised by the world,
Has a wondrous attraction for me;
For the dear Lamb of God
Left His glory above,
To bear it to dark Calvary.

In the old rugged cross,
Stained with blood so divine,
Such a wonderful beauty I see;
For 'twas on that old cross
Jesus suffered and died
To pardon and sanctify me.

—"The Old Rugged Cross" by George Bennard

Write out your thoughts about the overcoming life. What new understanding do
you have? How will it change your outlook?

_____

_____

_____

_____

_____

_____

_____

_____

_____

_____

_____

_____

_____

_____

_____

_____

_____

THE RESURRECTION LIFE

DAY ONE

Let's re-cap last week's lesson. For the first *adam* (Adam and Eve as a unit), the Tree of Life became a tree of death. Once they sinned, their physical bodies became containers of death, the "not-life." God's act of mercy barred Adam from eating of the Tree of Life so that he would not live forever in his physical body, his "body of death."

In Christ, our "body of death" or "body of sin" is done away with (Romans 6:6; Romans 7:24). We die to our old nature and are resurrected to new life. Our bodies, which used to be death-containers, are now life-containers.

▼

Review the thoughts from last week and solidify the concepts before you look at this week's material.

Define the word *overcome*.

What did Jesus overcome on our behalf?

How did Jesus overcome the world (sin, Satan, death)?

What was His job as the last Adam?

What was the enemy's scheme for bringing Jesus' mission to failure?

How did the enemy's scheme work to bring God's purpose to its fulfillment?

What did God use to perfect the soul of the last Adam?

What does the word *perfect* (either as a noun or as a verb) mean?

How do you overcome the enemy by the blood of the Lamb and the word of your testimony?

Parse the meaning of this verse. Dissect its phrases and restate them in your own words. *"I have been crucified with Christ and I no longer live, but Christ lives in me. The life I live in the body, I live by faith in the Son of God, who loved me and gave himself for me"* (Galatians 2:20).

I	
have been crucified	
with Christ	
and I no longer live	
but Christ lives in me	
The life I live in the body	
I live by faith in the Son of God	

All that I inherited from the first Adam—the Adam-life with Adam's spiritual DNA—has been crucified with Christ. Nevertheless, I live. Yet not I, but Christ in me. The life that is in me now is eternal life, Jesus Christ Himself (Galatians 2:20). He is eternal life and He is in me.

In John 15:5, Jesus uses the earth-visual of vine and branch to illustrate this spiritual truth. I am cut off from the not-life and grafted into the life. *"I am the vine; you are the branches. If a man remains in me and I in him, he will bear much fruit; apart from me you can do nothing."*

"If you remain," He says. In other words, "If the graft takes . . . ." He is using language that implies a branch that has been grafted into the vine. This means that the branch used to be part of a different vine. It started out attached to another source. I have been cut off from my old life and grafted into my new life. I used to be attached to the not-life vine, the Adam vine; now I am attached to the life-vine.

When the graft takes, the life in the vine becomes the life that flows through the branch. The branch has no other life except the vine's life. Whatever flows through the vine, now flows through the branch. The life in the vine and the life in the branch are one and the same. The vine's life circulates through the branch like blood circulates through my body.

SOUL AND FLESH

When God created humans, He created them with a soul. The soul is the human mind, will, and emotions. In the beginning, the human soul was innocent, neither good nor bad. Adam and Eve had a sinless version of the soul before the fall. Jesus, the last Adam, when He "became flesh," had a sinless version of the soul.

"The flesh," in general, refers to the operation of the human soul through the human body. Our "flesh" is sinful and unable to submit to God's law. It is a corrupted, polluted soul, carrying the sin-gene.

"Those who live according to the sinful nature have their minds set on what that nature desires; but those who live in accordance with the Spirit have their minds set on what the Spirit desires. The mind of sinful man is death, but the mind controlled by the Spirit is life and peace; the sinful mind is hostile to God. It does not submit to God's law, nor can it do so. Those controlled by the sinful nature cannot please God." —Romans 8:5–8

When the first Adam sinned, he allowed the functions of his soul (thinking, willing, and desiring) to take supremacy over the functions of his spirit (to worship and obey God; to allow God to be his source). Not only did sin put mankind in conflict with God, but it also put mankind in conflict with himself. Now his spirit, soul, and body were out of sync. Rather than working in tandem, as one integrated whole—in the image of Triune God: Father, Son, and Spirit—body, soul, and spirit began to operate in opposition to each other. Paul describes the sin condition in Romans 7.

"I do not understand what I do. For what I want to do I do not do, but what I hate I do. And if I do what I do not want to do, I agree that the law is good. . . .

"For I have the desire to do what is good, but I cannot carry it out. For what I do is not the good I want to do; no, the evil I do not want to do—this I keep on doing. . . .

"So I find this law at work: When I want to do good, evil is right there with me. For in my inner being I delight in God's law; but I see another law at work in the members of my body, waging war against the law of my mind and making me a prisoner of the law of sin at work within my members." —Romans 7:15–16, 18–19, 21–23

Paul concludes this passage with these words: *"Who will rescue me from this body of death?"* (Romans 7:24). He has just described what it is like to live in a death-container. He has just described the state of living death from which Jesus, the life, will rescue us.

Adam corrupted the soul and put it in bondage to sin and death. Since the fall, every descendant of Adam has been born with a corrupted soul. Each of us is born with a sin-gene in our spiritual DNA, which makes it certain that each of us will sin.

"Therefore, just as sin entered the world through one man, and death through sin, and in this way death came to all men, because all sinned . . . the many died by the trespass of the one man . . . as through the disobedience of the one man the many were made sinners" (Romans 5:12, 15, 19).

Just as Adam corrupted the soul and put it in bondage to sin and death, Jesus perfected the soul and freed it from sin and death.

"Who will rescue me from this body of death? Thanks be to God—through Jesus Christ our Lord!" —Romans 7:24–25

"For just as through the disobedience of the one man the many were made sinners, so also through the obedience of the one man the many will be made righteous." —Romans 5:19

DAY TWO

JESUS PERFECTED THE SOUL

Jesus had "flesh," but His flesh was sinless. It was not corrupted or polluted. Remember that through the process of His earth-life, Jesus was moving toward the moment when He would be *"the source of eternal salvation for all who obey him"* (Hebrews 5:9).

Jesus progressively matured, just as all humans do. He experienced all the developmental stages. *"And the child grew and became strong; he was filled with wisdom, and the grace of God was upon him"* (Luke 2:40). The Greek word translated "grew" indicates a progressive growth. It is the same word used to describe the growth of plants. It is in the imperfect tense, which indicates continuous action in the past. The phrase "was filled" is in a Greek tense that indicates a continuous or repeated action. Jesus went through a process of maturing. He grew, stage by stage, becoming progressively stronger. He was continuously being filled with wisdom.

At each stage, He matured in His obedience. *"Although he was a son, he learned obedience from what he suffered and, once made perfect, he became the source of eternal salvation to all who obey him"* (Hebrews 5:8–9).

Each new step of maturity brought with it a new level of obedience. He continued to learn by experience how to obey until He was ready to face the ultimate obedience. He became "obedient to the point of death, even death on a cross" (Philippians 2:8 NASB). His hand-to-hand combat against sin intensified at each stage until its climax at the cross.

At each step of the way, He was under the mastery of His spirit—the opposite of Adam's action. Remember that He was overcoming sin on our behalf. He was creating in His life the antibodies against sin so that He could transfuse us with His overcoming life.

Looking again at the earth-picture—the creation of antibodies in the blood—we see the spiritual truth. Recently I watched a program that detailed how scientists in South America develop the antidotes to counteract the venom of the many deadly poisonous snakes that live in their regions. To create the antidote, they first milk the venom from the snake. Then they inject a diluted form of that venom into a horse. Each day they inject an increased concentration of the venom until they are injecting the horse with undiluted venom. The horse's bloodstream is progressively developing antibodies against the venom. Once the horse's bloodstream has created immunity to the full-strength dose of venom, they draw that blood and use the horse's antibodies to create the antidote.

Do you see what the horse was doing? It was *becoming* the source of salvation (healing) for anyone who would be injected with its antibodies.

Dr. Paul Brand tells this story in his book *In His Image*:

Some years ago an epidemic of measles struck Vellore and one of my daughters had a severe attack. We knew she would recover, but our other infant daughter, Estelle, was dangerously vulnerable because of her age. When the pediatrician explained our need for convalescent serum, word went around Vellore that the Brands needed the "blood of an overcomer." We did not actually use those words, but we called for someone who had contracted measles and had overcome it. Serum from such a person would protect our little girl.

It was no use finding someone who had conquered chicken pox or had recovered from a broken leg. Such people, albeit healthy, could not give the specific help we needed to overcome measles. We needed someone who had experienced measles and had defeated that disease. We located such a person, withdrew some of his blood, let the cells settle out, and injected the

convalescent serum. Equipped with "borrowed" antibodies, our daughter fought off the disease successfully. . . . She overcame measles not by her own resistance or vitality, but as a result of a battle that had taken place previously within someone else.

—From *In His Image*, by Paul Brand and Philip Yancey

Do you see the picture? Jesus, in His earth-body and through His man-soul, was exposed to the ever-increasing temptations of Satan. Each victory furthered the process of developing the antidote to sin—not for Him, but for us. He was doing the work *for us*. What we could not do, He did for us.

The pictures of spiritual reality that God has painted into creation are only pictures. Early in the study I stated that a picture of an object is not the object. A picture is flat and one-dimensional and falls short of representing the reality perfectly. In this analogy, the picture falls short in that Jesus never was infected with the sin disease. He was exposed to the germ, but the disease never took hold, just as the horse is not overcome with the initial injection of snake venom. It is only enough to activate the creation of the destroyers (antibodies), not enough to poison the horse. Each progressively stronger injection only creates more antigens until the horse can withstand an undiluted dose of poison, so developed are the antibodies in its blood.

When Jesus transfuses us with His blood, it is His blood, not just an element of His blood added to ours. Here the analogy falls short again. His blood replaces our blood.

"For what the Law could not do, weak as it was through the flesh, God did: sending His own Son in the likeness of sinful flesh and as an offering for sin. He condemned sin in the flesh." —Romans 8:3 NASB

What could the Law not do?

Why could the Law not do it?

What did God do?

How did God do it?

▲

Paul states that God sent Jesus "in the likeness of sinful flesh." Jesus' soul had no taint of sin in it at the beginning, and He never yielded to temptation, whereby His soul would have become tainted by sin. But Paul is making a very clear statement here that Jesus had the same kind of soul that we have. He had a soul through which sin can enter. This is why He was able to fight our battle for us.

"He condemned sin in the flesh, so that the requirement of the Law might be fulfilled in us" (Romans 8:3–4 NASB). He took on flesh in order to "condemn sin in the flesh"—or beat Satan on his home turf. The word *condemned* has the sense of dethroning or deposing. The Law was able to pass judgment on sin, but only Jesus Himself could overthrow sin's dominion. A. T. Robertson explains that the Greek grammatical construct in this phrase yields this concept: "He condemned the sin of men and the condemnation took place in the flesh of Jesus."

Once He had dethroned sin in His flesh, that life could be transfused into us so that the Law might be fulfilled *in us*. During his earth-life, He did for us what the Law could not do. He did it in the flesh, through a man-soul. Then He came to live His victorious, sin-immune life in us.

Jesus came to earth as a man. He lived out His time on earth wrapped in flesh—a man-soul acting through an earth-body. That was the arena in which He overcame sin. He condemned sin *in His flesh*.

DAY THREE

JESUS' SOUL WAS THE SERVANT OF THE SPIRIT

Jesus' human spirit was the dwelling place of the Father. He was filled and empowered by the Holy Spirit. His obedience was in keeping His man-soul subjected to the indwelling Spirit. His man-soul was operating through His earth-body, but the Spirit of God was acting through His man-soul. "It is the Father living in me doing His work." Each temptation was an effort to get Jesus to act in the power of His flesh rather than in the power of the Spirit.

Even when He offered Himself on the cross, He was acting in the power of the Spirit. *"How much more, then, will the blood of Christ, who through the eternal Spirit offered himself unblemished to God, cleanse our consciences from acts that lead to death, so that we may serve the living God!"* (Hebrews 9:14).

Satan could not have tempted Him to do evil because, being holy, evil held no allure for Him. But Satan could tempt Him to do good in the flesh—not because Jesus wanted to sin, but because He wanted to do good. The Son of Man had to be able to divide between soul and spirit (Hebrews 4:12). For Jesus, with

His flesh-limitations, to resist Satan's subtle, skillful temptations, Jesus had to be in unbroken fellowship with the Father. He had to keep His steps synchronized with the Father's heart.

Jesus, though He was God and had always been God, voluntarily laid aside His independent power as God and limited Himself to flesh. He had the body and the soul of a man. He overcame sin as a man depending upon the power of the Father living in Him.

WISE BLOOD

The term sometimes used for blood that has immunity in it is "wise blood." The more times a person's bloodstream has been exposed to a particular invader and has overcome it, the more resistant the person becomes. Eventually, the person will become totally immune. The invader will have no effect.

From early childhood well into my college years, I was extremely sensitive to poison ivy. I really think I sometimes caught it just from hearing the words "poison ivy." Numerous times each year I was covered with blisters from head to foot from poison ivy. But now, I have not had poison ivy in more than 25 years. I can stand in the middle of it and not have any reaction. When it comes to poison ivy, I have "wise blood."

Jesus has "wise blood." He is making it available to you. Because of Him, you can have wise blood in your spirit-veins.

Read the following passage from the prophet Isaiah, describing the Messiah.

"Yet it was the LORD's will to crush him and cause him to suffer,
    and though the LORD makes his life a guilt offering,
he will see his offspring and prolong his days,
    and the will of the LORD will prosper in his hand.
After the suffering of his soul,
    he will see the light of life and be satisfied;
by his knowledge my righteous servant will justify many,
    and he will bear their iniquities.
Therefore I will give him a portion among the great,
    and he will divide the spoils with the strong,
because he poured out his life unto death,
    and was numbered with the transgressors.
For he bore the sin of many,
    and made intercession for the transgressors."
—Isaiah 53:10–12

Why do you think it was the Lord's will to "crush him and cause him to suffer"?

Describe how Jesus' life was being offered up as a guilt offering from His birth to His death.

Because He was willing to be offered up as a guilt offering for you and me, what are the three benefits He enjoys? Explain each in light of the blood of Christ.

Explain "the suffering of his soul" in the context of His task as the last Adam.

Following the suffering of His soul, as a result of the suffering of His soul, what has occurred?

What does it mean that He "poured out his *life* unto *death*"?

He will "divide the spoils with the strong." What are "spoils"? How does one get "spoils"? What are the "spoils" that Jesus won through battle?

What does it mean that He will "divide the spoils"? The word *divide* means "to share." Who will get a share of that which He alone won?

His job as the last Adam was to keep His flesh in its proper position: a servant of the Spirit. When every last battle had been fought, when Jesus' man-soul had been fully tested, then the next step toward the blood transfusion could begin.

DAY FOUR

THE CIRCUMCISION OF CHRIST

"In Him you were also circumcised with a circumcision made without hands, in the removal of the body of the flesh by the circumcision of Christ." —Colossians 2:11 NASB

Our God is a covenant God. Each time He bound Himself in covenant to His people, the covenant was ratified by the shedding of blood. Throughout the Old Testament, the picture-book, God initiated a series of covenants, each of which was a shadow of the true covenant, which would be *in* the blood of Jesus (Luke 22:20).

In the Old Testament covenants, the blood that was shed to seal the covenant was the blood of animals. There is one exception. There is one covenant in which the blood was shed by men. This was the covenant of circumcision.

This account is found in Genesis 17:1–11. Read the account and identify the two promises that the covenant of circumcision would seal.

The covenant promises from God were to Abraham. He promised that He would greatly increase the number of Abraham's descendants and that He would give Abraham and his descendants the land of Canaan as a possession. Then God said, *"You are to undergo circumcision, and it will be the sign of the covenant between me and you"* (Genesis 17:11). The physical act of circumcision was the cutting off of the foreskin, or the flesh. It was, as we will see, a picture of the crucifixion and resurrection of Christ.

"In Him you were also circumcised with a circumcision made without hands, in the removal of the body of the flesh by the circumcision of Christ; having been buried with Him in baptism, in which you were also raised up with Him through

faith in the working of God, who raised Him from the dead. When you were dead in your transgressions and the uncircumcision of your flesh, He made you alive together with Him, having forgiven us all our transgressions" (Colossians 2:11–13 NASB).

Paul writes that your "body of flesh" was removed "by the circumcision of Christ."

First, "body of flesh" in this passage is another way of saying "body of death" or "body of sin," which I have previously explained. Your flesh and my flesh is corrupted flesh. We inherited it from Adam. It is sinful flesh. Our flesh is our human soul acting apart from the divine influence.

▼

Define "body of flesh/ sin/ death" as you understand it.

▲

Our body of flesh is removed "by the circumcision of Christ." The phrase means "the circumcision that belongs to Christ." What is Christ's circumcision? Is Paul referring to Jesus' circumcision as an eight-day-old infant? Clearly not. One obvious clue is that Paul is referring to Jesus as "Christ." You will find that when the New Testament writers refer to Him as "Christ" rather than "Jesus," they are speaking of Him in His role as Messiah. The circumcision of Christ is an act of shedding blood (circumcision is a shedding of blood) in His role as Messiah.

Notice that Paul moves from "the circumcision of Christ" to the burial of Christ and to the resurrection of Christ.

"In Him you were also [1] circumcised with a circumcision made without hands, in the removal of the body of the flesh by the circumcision of Christ; having been [2] buried with Him in baptism, in which you were also [3] raised up with Him through faith in the working of God, who raised Him from the dead."

Compare that passage to Romans 6:2–4:

"We died to sin; how can we live in it any longer? Or don't you know that all of us who were baptized into Christ Jesus [1] were baptized into his death? We were therefore [2] buried with him through baptism into death in order that, just as Christ was [3] raised from the dead through the glory of the Father, we too may live a new life."

The symbol of *circumcision* in Colossians 2:11 is standing in the place of what reality?

He says that you were *circumcised* in Christ, then *buried* with Him, then *resurrected* with Him. This thought progression shows that Paul is putting the "circumcision of Christ" in the place of the crucifixion of Christ. Let's carefully examine how the covenant of circumcision is a picture of the crucifixion. The crucifixion of Christ, completed by His resurrection, was the reality that circumcision shadowed.

JESUS' FLESH

From His birth in Bethlehem until His physical death on the cross, Jesus was limited to flesh: the body and the soul of a man. His earth-body had to obey the earth-rules. For example, His earth-body was subject to the laws of gravity and of time and space. He could not be two places at once. He got tired and hungry. He felt physical pain. He could not go back and forth between heaven and earth.

Of course, there were moments when His earth-body seemed able to suspend the laws of earth. He walked on the water, for example. But those were not the norm. Those were moments when the Father, living in Him, overruled the laws of earth.

We know that He had limited Himself to a man-soul. He only knew what His Father told Him. His Father showed Him what to do. He drew His power from the Holy Spirit. He was led by the Spirit. He did not operate in His own power as God, but instead operated by the power of the Father manifested through Him.

"I tell you the truth, the Son can do nothing by himself; he can do only what he sees his Father doing." —John 5:19

"By myself I can do nothing." —John 5:30

"When you have lifted up the Son of Man, then you will know that I am the one I claim to be and that I do nothing on my own but speak just what the Father has taught me." —John 8:28

When Jesus was crucified, it was His earth-body that bled and died. It was His man-soul that cried out in anguish. It was His earth-body that was taken down from the cross, wrapped in grave clothes, and laid in the tomb.

After the resurrection, though, all of the limitations of His earth-body and His man-soul were left in the grave. He could move at will between the spiritual realm and the material realm. He could walk through walls. His resurrection body was not subject to the laws of earth. He was buried in His earth-body, but was resurrected in His heavenly body. His flesh was cut off. He was circumcised.

Where did Jesus carry our sins? Read Romans 7:4 and 1 Peter 2:24.

Where did Jesus carry our sins? In His body!

"*You also died to the law through the body of Christ*" (Romans 7:4).

"*He himself bore our sins in his body on the tree*" (1 Peter 2:24).

In these verses, the Greek word for "body" is *soma*. It specifically means the physical body or carcass. It was His *soma* that was removed from the cross and His *soma* that was placed in the tomb. When Christ was circumcised—when His flesh was cut off—your sins were cut off and thrown away. The physical earth-body—the *soma*—of Jesus no longer exists, and *neither do your sins*. That old "you" was crucified with Christ. You have been circumcised with the circumcision of Christ.

Define what it means to be circumcised with the circumcision of Christ.

What does it mean to you to know that your sins have been cut off and thrown away?

Resurrection life is a life that has been circumcised with the circumcision of Christ.

DAY FIVE

A NEW BODY WITH NEW BLOOD

For a time, Jesus' life was contained in an earth-body that God had prepared for Him (Hebrews 10:5). His life was something separate from His body, but was contained in and expressed through His body. During that period of time the life was limited to that one and only physical vehicle.

When Jesus was resurrected, His earth-body no longer existed. The tomb was empty. He rose from the dead in His spiritual body—a body no longer limited to the laws of the material realm. He was no longer limited to a man-soul. All of His flesh—earth-body and man-soul—was cut off. He was circumcised.

In His resurrected body, only pure Spirit-blood ran through His veins. Apparently, His body looked like an earth-body to the naked eye. It even retained His wounds. But one thing was radically different. He said to His disciples, when they were startled at His presence because they thought He was dead: *"Look at my hands and my feet. It is I myself! Touch me and see; a ghost does not have flesh and bones, as you see I have"* (Luke 24:39). Flesh and bones, but no blood. His resurrected body had no earth-life in it. Only eternal life flowed through Him. His earth-life had been cut off.

When that earth-vehicle, the body of the man Jesus, was destroyed, the life it contained was no longer limited to one body. When Jesus finished with His earth-body, when His flesh was circumcised, the resurrection life became available to all believers to dwell in their earth-bodies.

Andrew Murray says, "The life in him and in us is the same. Christ is our life."

Jesus lives in me as the resurrection and the life. The life He transfuses into my spirit-veins has accomplished for me everything that I could not do for myself. The life has already overcome sin and died to the power of the flesh. The life has brought the flesh back into its proper position, making it the servant of the Spirit.

He is God's everything. It all depends on Him. Apart from Him, I can do nothing. I have nothing to offer, except His life in me.

Circumcised with the Circumcision of Christ

Remember the original covenant of circumcision. God promised Abraham that He would make him fruitful and increase his numbers and that God would give Abraham and his descendants the land of Canaan. Circumcision was the sign of the covenant.

"The promises were spoken to Abraham and to his seed. The Scripture does not say 'and to seeds,' meaning many people, but 'and to your seed,' meaning one person, who is Christ." —Galatians 3:16

"If you belong to Christ, then you are Abraham's seed, and heirs according to the promise." —Galatians 3:29

"For those God foreknew he also predestined to be conformed to the likeness of his Son, that he might be the firstborn among many brothers." —Romans 8:29

How does the real circumcision—the crucifixion and resurrection of Jesus—fulfill the covenant? The fruitfulness promised Abraham is fulfilled in Christ. It is through His circumcision at the cross that the covenant promise is brought into its fullness. His resurrection life dwells in multitudes of believers. He is the firstborn among many brothers.

In the third and fourth chapters of Hebrews, we discover that Jesus is the Promised Land, the land of rest. Because of His resurrection life, the life that has subdued flesh and conquered sin, we have access to all the promises of God. He is our dwelling place. We are at home and at rest in Him. The promise of an eternal land to possess is fulfilled because Jesus' circumcision was begun at the cross and completed at His resurrection. When He rose from the dead, His flesh had been cut off. Now His resurrection life is available to me. I can dwell in the land of rest, the Kingdom of God.

"Don't you know that all of us who were baptized into Christ Jesus were baptized into his death? We were therefore buried with him through baptism into death in order that, just as Christ was raised from the dead through the glory of the Father, we too may live a new life.

"If we have been united with him like this in his death, we will certainly also be united with him in his resurrection. For we know that our old self was crucified with him so that the body of sin might be done away with, that we should no longer be slaves to sin—because anyone who has died has been freed from sin."
—Romans 6:3–7

The word *baptize* means "to become one with; to be immersed in." We are united with Him in His crucifixion; and we are united with Him in His resurrection.

How can you and I have been united with Him in His crucifixion if we weren't even born yet? Scripture gives us a hint of how God sees the crucifixion in the book of Hebrews. Notice how the writer of Hebrews makes this case. It will seem unrelated at first glance, but stay with me.

"This Melchizedek was king of Salem and priest of God Most High. He met Abraham returning from the defeat of the kings and blessed him, and Abraham gave him a tenth of everything. First, his name means 'king of righteousness'; then also, 'king of Salem' means 'king of peace.' Without father or mother, without genealogy, without beginning of days or end of life, like the Son of God he remains a priest forever.

"Just think how great he was: Even the patriarch Abraham gave him a tenth of the plunder! Now the law requires the descendants of Levi who become priests to collect a tenth from the people—that is, their brothers—even though their brothers are descended from Abraham. This man, however, did not trace his descent from Levi, yet he collected a tenth from Abraham and blessed him who had the promises. And without doubt the lesser person is blessed by the greater. In the one case, the tenth is collected by men who die; but in the other case, by him who is declared to be living. One might even say that Levi, who collects the tenth, paid the tenth **through Abraham,** *because when Melchizedek met Abraham,* **Levi was still in the body of his ancestor."** —Hebrews 7:1–10

The writer is telling a story about when Abraham paid a tithe to a man named Melchizedek. The point he is making is that Levi (from whom the tribe of priests is descended) actually paid the tithe "through Abraham." His reasoning is that because one day, many generations in the future, Levi would be born of the line of Abraham, Levi was "in the body of his ancestor." God saw you in the body of Christ when He hung on the cross. It was as if you died.

The spiritual realm is not governed by linear time. God saw you in Christ even before the world began. Because you would one day be "born again" of the Spirit, you were in Christ at His crucifixion.

You have been crucified with Christ. If the truth of it is just now becoming reality for you and just now changing you perceptions, that does not change the fact that it has always been so. When Jesus died on the cross, He bore your sins in His body.

Jesus surrendered Himself to the crucifixion. He purposefully kept His flesh in subjection to His spirit right up to the point of His death.

His lifeless *soma* was laid in a tomb. For three days it lay dead. For three days, there was no life in His *soma*. Then, at the ripe and appointed moment, the Spirit entered into Him and put life into His body. And His body was changed. It no longer had the molecular, cellular makeup of earth-stuff. The resurrection transformed the body of the Lord Jesus and transferred Him from earth to heaven. Even though He appeared for forty days on planet earth, He was part of the spiritual realm, not the material realm. His flesh no longer existed and does not exist to this day.

Write out Romans 8:9–11.

When Jesus was resurrected, who is it that put life into His body?

Who has put life into your mortal body? What kind of life is it?

What does this tell you about resurrection life?

Jesus entered willingly into His crucifixion. Then the resurrection entered into Him. In the same way, I enter into His crucifixion. I let my flesh go to the cross. I die to my old ways of thinking and acting. When I do, His resurrection life enters into me. I am united with Him in His death and I am united with Him in His resurrection.

His life in me is His flesh-free, sin-conquering, victorious life. It is His resurrection life. First Corinthians 15:45 tells us that the last Adam is a life-giving Spirit.

"If the Spirit of him who raised Jesus from the dead is living in you, he who raised Christ from the dead will also give life to your mortal bodies through his Spirit, who lives in you." —Romans 8:11

The very Spirit who raised Jesus from the dead lives in me. In Him, my flesh is cut off. I am circumcised with the circumcision of Christ.

REFLECT

When Jesus died and rose again, your sins were cut off. Let the truth of it penetrate your heart. The secret to experiencing your freedom is to remember *who Christ is in you*. The resurrection. The life.

The power of the blood is continually flowing through you—the blood with the antidote to everything that afflicts you. The blood has the resurrection in it. In you! Your soul can be in continual contact with all the power in the blood!

Would you be free from the burden of sin?
There's pow'r in the blood, pow'r in the blood.
Would you o'er evil a victory win?
There's wonderful pow'r in the blood.

Would you be free from your passion and pride?
There's pow'r in the blood, pow'r in the blood.
Come for a cleansing to Calvary's tide;
There's wonderful pow'r in the blood.

Would you be whiter, much whiter than snow?
There's pow'r in the blood, pow'r in the blood.
Sin stains are lost in its life-giving flow;
There's wonderful pow'r in the blood.

— "There Is Power in the Blood" by Lewis E. Jones

Write out your statement of faith regarding the resurrection life of Christ in you. Put the whole spiritual realm on notice—there is power in the blood!

_____

_____

_____

_____

_____

_____

_____

_____

_____

_____

_____

_____

_____

_____

_____

_____

_____

_____

THE CLEANSING LIFE

DAY ONE

THE TWOFOLD FUNCTION OF THE BLOOD

Write out 1 John 1:9. Circle or underline the phrases that indicate that the Father will deal with sin in two ways.

How did He provide for forgiveness of our sinful actions?

How did He provide for purifying of our unrighteousness?

The Father will deal with us in two ways: He will forgive our sins and He will purify us from all unrighteousness. By what method? God has only one delivery system for His power and provision: the blood of Christ: "the blood of Jesus, his Son, purifies us from all sin" (1 John 1:7). Just as your body has only one delivery system for power or cleansing, so the blood of Christ is the one and only provision for power and cleansing in the spiritual realm. Clay Trumbull refers to the blood of Christ this way: "the sacrificial offering which could supply to [man's] death-smitten nature the vivifying blood of an everlasting covenant" (H. Clay Trumbull, *The Blood Covenant*).

▼

Read Romans 5:10. Write out the phrases that point us to the two-fold role of the blood in our complete salvation:

1.

2.

▲

Through the blood, God will deal with our sins by forgiving them, and He will deal with the unrighteousness that causes us to sin by cleansing it. Do you remember in the first lesson that we identified two roles of Jesus' blood in our salvation? (Romans 5:10):

1. His earth-blood was spilled out for payment of sin: *"We were reconciled to him through the death of his Son."*

2. His Spirit-blood was poured out in the heavenly tabernacle and now runs through your spirit-veins: *"How much more, having been reconciled, shall we be saved through his life!"*

By His shedding of blood on the cross, He provided for the forgiveness of our sins. His blood works God-ward. We are reconciled to God by the death of His Son.

Through the continuously flowing fountain of His blood through us, He provides an ongoing cleansing from unrighteousness. How does blood cleanse? It cleanses by flowing through. The verb tense in 1 John 1:7 indicates continuous or repeated action. His blood continually purifies us from all unrighteousness. His blood works in us, bringing new life. His blood works us-ward. We are saved by His life.

"For God was pleased to have all his fullness dwell in him, and through him to reconcile to himself all things, whether things on earth or things in heaven, by making peace through his blood, shed on the cross" (Colossians 1:19–20). The word *reconcile* means to bring together two separate things and make the two into one. Paul writes in Colossians that God has reconciled us to Himself through the blood of Christ. He interchanges the terms *reconcile* and *make peace*. Paul elaborates on his thought: *"Once you were alienated from God and were enemies in your minds because of your evil behavior. But now he has reconciled you by Christ's physical body through death to present you holy in his sight, without blemish and free from accusation"* (Colossians 1:21–22). There was a time when you and God were separated, but now you are reconciled. The meaning goes much further than, "Now you have settled all your disagreements." The Hebrew for "peace" is *shalom*, which means "wholeness." Paul is actually saying, "Now you are one. Once you were alienated from each other, but now you are reconciled to each other. Once you were two, but now you are one." How did you become one? By the blood of Jesus, the blood that His death on the cross made available.

The word translated "reconcile" is the equivalent of the Hebrew word for "atone." I'm certain that Paul, with his strong Jewish roots, was speaking in language and metaphors that intentionally reproduced the language of the Old Covenant, translating its meaning in light of the New Covenant. He meant for his readers to hear the echo of the ceremonial laws of temple sacrifices in his statements.

Under the Old Covenant, there were two blood sacrifices that resulted in "atonement." These were the sin offering and the guilt offering, sometimes called the trespass offering. I don't want to bog you down here in Hebrew words and technicalities of the Jewish sacrificial system, but I think you will be enriched by the instruction (Hebrew: *torah*) hidden in the details. I'm going to keep it as uncomplicated as possible, but stick with me. The riches are stored in the secret places.

There were two kinds of sacrifices. One was called the "bringing near" (*korban*) and the other was the "offering up" (*ola*). The "binging near" offering was brought near by the sinner. The person making the sacrifice did the slaughtering himself or herself. (Yes, women made their own offerings.) It was also understood that the "bringing near" offering brought the person back into relationship with God—brought him or her "near" to God. The sin offering and the guilt offering were the two "bringing near" sacrifices.

The "offering up" sacrifices, just as point of reference, were made *after* the "bringing near" offerings and were offerings of worship, joy, communion. Alfred Edersheim explains: "These were, then, either sacrifices of communion with God, or else [were] intended to restore that communion when it had been disturbed or dimmed through sin and trespass: sacrifices *in* communion with God, or [sacrifices] *for* communion with God. To the former class [*in* communion] belong the burnt and the peace offering; to the latter [*for* communion], the sin and the trespass offerings" (*The Temple, Its Ministry and Service*; I have added the bracketed words for clarification).

We want to concentrate on the sin offering and the guilt offerings, the two "bringing near" sacrifices. You will see that these two blood sacrifices perfectly shadow the two-fold function of the blood of Christ.

SIN OFFERING

The sin offering (Leviticus 4:1–5, 13, 6: 24–30; 8:14–17; 16:3–22) was offered as a general cleansing from defilement. The word is *hattat*. It means "pollution, contamination." According to Everett Fox, "The *hattat* decontaminates the sanctuary, and apparently individuals as well. . . . Central to the *hattat*-offering is the use of its blood to absorb and purify the pollution that has accrued in the sanctuary" (*The Five Books of Moses*). The blood of the sin offering purified a worshiper of his or her general state of pollution. The blood of our *hattat*-offering, Jesus Christ, purifies us of all unrighteousness.

THE GUILT OFFERING

The guilt offering (Leviticus 5:14–6:7; 7:1–6) was offered for specific actions. The Hebrew word is *asham* and means acts of sin. In the guilt offering, the sinner is aware of the sin and the damage that sin has done. He might have committed the sin unknowingly, but once he becomes aware of it, he is required to bring a guilt offering and also to make restitution. (In contrast, the sin offering makes atonement for sins that the offerer does not even know he or she has committed.) The blood of the *asham*-offering pays for the sins and reconciles the sinner to God. The blood of our *asham*-offering, Jesus Christ, pays for our sins and reconciles us to the Father.

We have two problems: (1) sins and (2) unrighteousness. Sins are the behaviors we engage in. Unrighteousness is the attitude of rebellion that causes us to sin.

▼

Write out Zechariah 13:1.

The fountain of which Zechariah speaks is the blood of Christ. What purpose will this fountain serve? It will cleanse from _____ and

_____ .

▲

When Zechariah foretold that the fountain of His blood would flow, he prophesied that the fountain would be "to cleanse them from sin and impurity" (Zechariah

13:1). Jesus' blood is the complete remedy for both problems. Our sins are paid for by His death; our unrighteousness is being cleansed by His life. He is both our *hattat*-offering and our *asham*-offering.

Read Hebrews 10:1–4.

"The law is only a shadow of the good things that are coming—not the realities themselves. For this reason it can never, by the same sacrifices repeated endlessly year after year, make perfect those who draw near to worship. If it could, would they not have stopped being offered? For the worshipers would have been cleansed once for all, and would no longer have felt guilty for their sins. But those sacrifices are an annual reminder of sins, because it is impossible for the blood of bulls and goats to take away sins."

Do you see in this passage direct references to the two-fold function of the blood of Christ? Write out the phrases that point back to the shadow of the sacrificial system.

When you look at the shadow of something, the shadow appears to be pointed in the opposite direction of the reality it shadows. For example, if I stand so that my entire body casts a shadow, the shadow created by my right hand appears to be the shadow-figure's left hand.

The sin offering and the guilt offering are the shadows cast by the most beautiful reality of all. It shadows redemption. In the sacrificial system, the sinner brought the blood. In the redemption, God brought the blood. In the sacrificial system, the sinner sought to come near to God. In redemption, God came near to the sinner. Jesus, our "bringing near" offering, has come near to us. His name says it all: Immanuel—God with us.

In the Old Covenant, when the sinner brought his or her sin offering or guilt offering, it was examined inside and out by the priest. The sinner was accepted on the basis of the perfection of his offering. The offerer himself was not examined; just his sacrifice.

Your "bringing near" offering has been deemed pure, undefiled, without spot or blemish, perfect. You can draw near to God because of the blood of the Lord Jesus.

"Therefore, brothers, since we have confidence to enter the Most Holy Place by the blood of Jesus, by a new and living way opened for us through the curtain, that

is, his body, and since we have a great priest over the house of God, let us draw near to God with a sincere heart in full assurance of faith, having our hearts sprinkled to cleanse us from a guilty conscience and having our bodies washed with pure water. Let us hold unswervingly to the hope we profess, for he who promised is faithful." —Hebrews 10:19–23

DAY TWO

THE FLESH

Even though I am born again of the Spirit and my spirit-marrow no longer manufactures Adam-life, I still have residual Adam-life flowing in my spirit-veins. It has not all been sloughed away yet. Little by little, from one degree of glory to the next, I am being changed: old things are passing away, new things are taking their place (2 Corinthians 3:18; 2 Corinthians 5:17).

This leftover Adam-life is called my "flesh." My flesh is any point at which I am not allowing the life to flow. My flesh is operating when my soul is in command rather than the Spirit of Christ in me. God is determined to flush all the flesh out of me. Flesh cannot be improved. Flesh cannot be corrected or made holy. It has to die. Flesh must be crucified.

God's goal is that the power of the resurrection will be manifested in your life. Keep in mind that the resurrection life of Christ is His present-tense life. The life He is living right now being expressed in you and through you (Romans 8:11). He is the Victor and His victorious, overcoming, eternal life is in you. God's purpose for you is that the resurrection life of Jesus will flow freely through you.

Here's the secret: It takes a crucifixion to experience a resurrection.

Because of His great love for you, the Father is building experiences into your life that will cause your flesh to come to the surface and be exposed. He is engineering circumstances and encounters that will engage your flesh. This is so that flesh can be surrendered to the crucifixion.

When you find yourself in a situation in which your flesh is exposed, you have come to what I call a "crucifixion moment." You can now choose to act and respond in the pattern of your flesh, or you can surrender that flesh to the cross. If you choose your flesh-pattern, you are cut off from the flow of resurrection life. If you choose the cross, the resurrection life flows. You have to let the crucifixion be manifested in your flesh if you want the resurrection to be manifested in your life. *"We always carry around in our body the death of Jesus, so that the life of Jesus may also be revealed in our body"* (2 Corinthians 4:10).

A crucifixion moment brings you to a choice. Just as Jesus chose the crucifixion and laid down His own life by His own choice, you, too, must choose crucifixion. You willingly enter into the crucifixion by denying your flesh, by not responding to its commands. When you do, the resurrection enters into you.

What leftover Adam-life is God bringing to your attention right now? What circumstances is He allowing that brings your flesh out into the open?

How will you change your perception of and your reaction to these circumstances so that old Adam-life can be sloughed away?

THE RESURRECTION LIFE

Jesus willingly laid down His life and then the Spirit raised Him from the dead. The resurrection entered into Him. If you are united with Him in His death, you are certainly also united with Him in His resurrection.

Examine this rich passage from Romans 8:9–11 with me, piece by piece.

"You, however, are controlled not by the sinful nature but by the Spirit, if the Spirit of God lives in you."

Change the word "if" to "since" and you will have a better sense of the meaning. Since the Spirit of God lives in you, you are not managed by and subject to the sinful nature: the flesh.

What is the Holy Spirit called here?

Where is the Holy Spirit living?

"And if anyone does not have the Spirit of Christ, he does not belong to Christ."

There is no middle ground. You do belong to Christ, therefore you do have the

Spirit of Christ living in you. What is the Holy Spirit called here?

Is this the same Holy Spirit who was just referred to as "the Spirit of God"?

"But if (since) *Christ is in you, your body is dead because of sin, yet your spirit is alive because of righteousness."*

What is Paul meaning to communicate when he says "your body is dead"? He is talking to an audience whose bodies are alive.

What is Paul contrasting? You body is becoming more dead, but what is happening to your spirit?

"And if the Spirit of him who raised Jesus from the dead is living in you, he who raised Christ from the dead will also give life to your mortal bodies through his Spirit, who lives in you."

Here the Holy Spirit is called "the Spirit of him who raised Jesus from the dead." Who raised Jesus from the dead? See Romans 10:9 and Romans 4:24.

Since the same Power who raised Jesus from the dead is now living in you, He is giving life to your mortal body. Paul is not talking about the resurrection that will occur at the end of time, because he says that the life is in your "mortal body." Your mortal body is your body that is subject to death, not your eternal body, which will be given you at the end of time and will not age, decay, or die. He uses the Greek word *soma* for "body," which means the carcass. Because of the life in you, the body you are walking around in is being animated by the same Spirit who raised Jesus from the dead.

Romans 10:9 says, *"If you confess with your mouth, 'Jesus is Lord,' and believe in your heart that God raised him from the dead, you will be saved"* (Romans 10:9). God the Father raised Jesus from the dead. Then read this: *"He was put to death in the body but made alive by the Spirit"* (1 Peter 3:18). The Holy Spirit raised Jesus from the dead.

Several important points are buried in these words, waiting to be mined like silver or gold. Each point will add more substance to your understanding of His life in you.

The Holy Spirit, the Spirit of Christ, and the Spirit of God are all names for one Being. God the Father, God the Son, and God the Spirit are one. They are not fragmented and separate, but instead are one integrated whole, three acting in such perfect harmony that they are one. Elohim, the Triune God, lives in you and acts through you.

Exactly the same Spirit who is in Jesus is in you. The life in Him and in you is the same life. You are united with Him in His resurrection. What does it mean to be united with Him? *"But the one who joins himself to the Lord is one spirit with Him"* (1 Corinthians 6:17 NASB).

In the material world, when two elements unite and become a solution, it means that their molecules merge and become one. What had been two separate elements have now become one single solution. If, for example, salt and water are combined, they become a new solution. You could say, "The salt molecule is in the water molecule." Or you could say, "The water molecule is in the salt molecule." You would be stating the same fact either way.

In the spiritual realm, you have become one Spirit with Christ. Christ is in you and you are in Christ. That is how fully one you now are. His resurrection is your resurrection.

The blood in your body, which is made up of red cells, white cells, and platelets, is suspended in a fluid called "serum," where their activity is carried out. All of those parts taken together as a whole are "blood." The Father, Son, and Spirit are actively living and working in you. Your being is the serum—the vehicle through which the Three-in-One is working. It takes all the parts to make the whole.

The power of His resurrection is not something for your future, but it is working in you now. The flesh that remains in you hinders the flow of resurrection life through you. The flesh is death; the Spirit is life. The flesh has to be removed so that you can experience all the power of His resurrection.

DAY THREE

EXPOSED FLESH

That flesh in us nourishes the root of unrighteousness that grows the sin-fruit. God is after the root. When the root is gone, the fruit will cease to exist.

"Woe to you, teachers of the law and Pharisees, you hypocrites! You clean the outside of the cup and dish, but inside they are full of greed and self-indulgence. Blind Pharisee! First clean the inside of the cup and dish, and then the outside also will be clean" (Matthew 23:25–26). Jesus said that when the inside is clean the outside will be clean. We spend our energy trying to get rid of sins, when God wants to uproot sin's source.

How does He do it? What is His method? Remember that the Father trained the Son in deeper levels of obedience by allowing temptation. He uses the same method with us. Although with Jesus He had no unrighteousness to uproot, there is still a similar process at work. He used temptation to bring Jesus to maturity, and He can use temptation to bring us to maturity. God is not doing the tempting, but He is using the temptation to perfect us. James writes that trials of various kinds will work to our advantage *"so that* [we] *may be mature and complete, not lacking anything"* (James 1:4).

▼

Stop now and read James 1:2, then verse 12, then verses 14 and 15. These will be the focal verses from which we will build and understanding of how God uses temptation to flush out flesh. Write out the verses.

James 1:2

James 1:12

James 1:14–15

▲

The Greek word translated "trials" in James 1:2 and again in verse 12 is the same word translated "tempt" in verses 14 and 15. The same Greek word is translated "test" in other passages. You realize that in Greek, just as in any language, there are certain words that though spelled the same, can mean different things depending on the context. Sometimes, then, it is a subjective decision made by the translators how to translate a certain word.

In verses 14 and 15, as we will see, the context is unmistakable. James is clearly talking about temptation to sin. The three bold-faced words in the following passage are all the same Greek word. It makes more sense to recognize that he is using the same word in a single passage consistently to mean the same thing: temptation.

*"Consider it pure joy, my brothers, whenever you face **trials** of many kinds, because you know that the **testing** of your faith develops perseverance. Perseverance must finish its work so that you may be mature and complete, not lacking anything."* —James 1:2–4

*"Blessed is the man who perseveres under **trial**, because when he has stood the test, he will receive the crown of life that God has promised to those who love him. When **tempted**, . . ."* —James 1:12-13

Strange as it may seem at first, I am convinced that James is saying, "Consider it pure joy, my brothers, whenever you face *temptations* of many kinds." Remember what a productive use God made of the temptations Jesus faced. Is it possible that He could use temptation to our advantage also?

▼

"God is faithful; he will not let you be tempted beyond what you can bear." —1 Corinthians 10:13

Who is in charge of what temptation reaches you?

What phrase in this verse indicates that God has final say about what temptation reaches you?

▲

In 1 Corinthians 10:13 we find the same Greek word for "tempt" as is found in our passage from James. Look carefully at what the Scripture says about temptation: God will not *let you be tempted* beyond what you can bear. Do you see that God is in charge of what temptation reaches you? If God is in charge of what temptation reaches you, can temptation have any purpose but good? *"All the ways of the LORD are loving and faithful for those who keep the demands of his covenant"* (Psalm 25:10). *"You are good, and what you do is good"* (Psalm 119:68).

God allows temptation in order to isolate, identify, and uproot unrighteousness and expose flesh.

Let me backtrack and clarify something. **God is not tempting you.** He is not the source of temptation. *"When tempted, no one should say, 'God is tempting me.' For God cannot be tempted by evil, nor does he tempt anyone"* (James 1:13). He, however, decides what temptation will be allowed to reach you.

▼

Why should we consider it pure joy when faced with temptations of many kinds?

Do you believe there is anything Satan devises that can outwit God?

Do you believe that Satan has the freedom to act without God's permission? (See Luke 22:31; Job 1:12)

Do you believe there are temptations Satan would like to bring your way for which God will not give him permission?

Do you believe that God has a plan for your life?

That He watches over you without intermission?

Does God know a temptation is headed your way before it reaches you?

What does He do in preparation? Read all of 1 Corinthians 10:13.

What good, productive purpose might God have in mind by allowing temptation?

DAY FOUR

THE ANATOMY OF A SIN

Temptation is not sin. Temptation does not have to lead to sin. However, no sin comes into being without temptation. What is the process by which temptation becomes sin? *"Each one is tempted when, by his own evil desire, he is dragged away and enticed. Then, after desire has conceived, it gives birth to sin"* (James 1:14–15). In this passage, James is talking about temptation that is successful, or results in sin. He describes for us the process.

Fill in the missing words in the phrases as we investigate the meaning.

"By his own e_____ d_____ . . ."

The Greek word translated "evil desire" really means strong or intense desire. It does not have a specific meaning of good or bad. In fact, it is the same word Jesus used in Luke 22:15 when He said to His disciples: *"I have **eagerly desired** to eat this Passover with you before I suffer."* In the phrase above, put an X through the word "evil" and write in "strong."

This strong or intense desire, at its foundation, is built into you by the Creator. He has created you with a deep need for love and acceptance *so that* you will seek and find love and acceptance in Him. This need is the foundation of every desire. However, our God-created desires become misdirected when we seek to have them met outside of God.

Anything outside of God only meets the surface of the need and provides only temporary relief and must be repeated over and over again. *"As when a hungry man dreams that he is eating, but he awakens, and his hunger remains; as when a thirsty man dreams that he is drinking, but he awakens faint, with his thirst unquenched"* (Isaiah 29:8). We spend our resources on bread, which does not satisfy. We devour, but are still hungry; we eat, but are not filled.

When we repeatedly turn our strong and intense desire outward to the world, a pattern of behavior becomes fixed. The very need or desire that should have turned us to God has turned us away from Him. Instead of being freed from our need by having it eternally met, we become enslaved to our need by having it forever unsatisfied. We have, then, a *misdirected desire*. It has taken root in us. It becomes a *root of unrighteousness* and it grows a fruit called sin.

"By his own [strong] desire, he is _____ _____ and _____." (James 1:14)

This misdirected desire, this root, has developed a magnetic attraction to something in the world. We'll call the object or situation in the world a "stimulus." A stimulus in the world acts as a magnet to entice you and drag you away. James is really using a fishing term here. It means "to bait" or "to set a trap." Satan has dangled bait in front of you. Your misdirected desire has taken the bait and been lured into a trap.

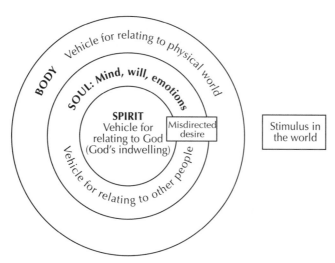

The stimulus has no power of its own. What tempts one person does not tempt another. The power is not in the object or the occurrence in the world. The stimulus is neutral. Unless it is enticing, it cannot tempt. Its only power is the attraction it holds for you. *It is your own misdirected desire dragging you away.*

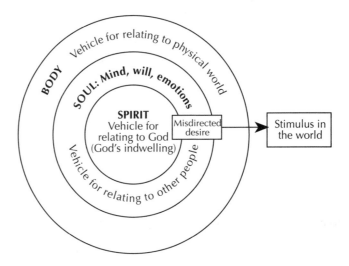

"After _____ has _____, it gives _____ to sin." (James 1:15)

The root of unrighteousness in you mates with the stimulus in the world. The mating results in conception, and sin is born. Sin is born of the mating between your misdirected desire and a stimulus in the world.

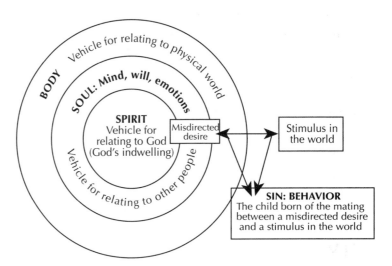

If one or the other (misdirected desire or stimulus in the world) did not exist, no mating could occur. It is unrealistic to think that the stimuli the world offers will disappear. Jesus said that we would have trouble in the world. He prayed that we not be removed from the world, but protected from its damaging influence. The stimuli in the world will not go away. Where does the answer lie?

The root of unrighteousness must be destroyed. Once the root is gone, the stimulus in the world has nothing to mate with. The stimulus loses its power and becomes a neutral object. *Once the inside is clean, the outside will be clean also.*

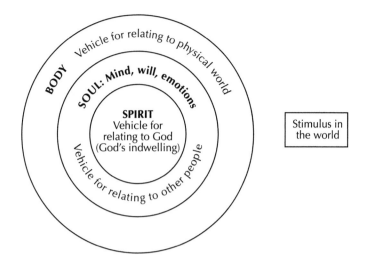

TEMPTATION THAT LEADS TO PURITY

Temptation can lead to sin, or temptation can lead to purity. Temptation forces choice. Every time we face temptation, we choose where to take our needs. Will we allow God to fulfill them and satisfy our eternal cravings? Or will we take the drive-through fast-food approach? Will we think long-term or quick fix? Will we choose God or will we choose Baal? Every temptation forces us deeper into the heart of the Father or anchors us more securely in the world.

In the same way that our flesh impulses became flesh-patterns by repeating an action over and over again, so temptation can cause us to become fixed in the way of the Spirit by persistent choice. We can choose Him over and over until He becomes our holy habit and the ways of the Spirit become our spontaneous choice.

Temptation shows us the places at which we are still responsive to sin. Temptation is a heart echogram. It pinpoints the weak places. It exposes flesh. Remember that the stimulus can only entice if a root of unrighteousness is present. Temptation exposes impurities. It unmasks our hearts so that sin cannot lurk there undetected. It exposes flesh and forces a crucifixion moment. Temptation forces flesh into the light where it can be destroyed.

DAY FIVE

THE CLEANSING LIFE

Jesus' blood dealt with not only sins, but also with the inner unrighteousness that produces sin.

"He was delivered over to death for our sins and was raised to life for our justification" (Romans 4:25).

Enclose in brackets each of the two parts of our salvation. What role does the blood of Christ play in each aspect of our salvation?

We are being saved every moment by his life. His blood flowing through our spirit-veins is flushing our flesh. Forgiveness of sins has been accomplished once for all at the cross. Purification from unrighteousness is an ongoing process—a process that is being accomplished by the Lord Himself. His Spirit-blood running through our spirit-veins carries away the flesh-toxins that poison us and produce symptoms in our lives: sinful behaviors. His life in us is uprooting the root that grows the fruit.

A SPIRITUAL TOURNIQUET

As blood flows through my body, what happens if I tie a tourniquet around my arm? At that place, the blood is not free to flow. Eventually, toxins build up because the blood-flow is not washing them away. Little by little, the part of my arm cut off from the blood withers and dies.

Flesh is like a spiritual tourniquet. Flesh cuts off the flow of life in you. As you obey, the tourniquet is removed and the cleansing life floods your spirit-cells.

Temptation warns you of spiritual tourniquets. Each time you yield yourself to the cleansing life in you, you loosen a tourniquet. Little by little, the tourniquet loses its hold on you. The key is to move your emphasis from focusing entirely on your behavior and turn toward the life in you, drawing on His finished work and the antibodies against sin.

Madame Guyon, in her book *Experiencing the Depths of Jesus Christ*, gives this advice:

Christians have sought to find many ways to overcome their desires. Perhaps the most common approach has been discipline and self-denial. But no matter how severe your self-denial may be, it will never completely conquer your senses. No, self-denial is not the answer!

Even when it appears to have worked, what self-denial has actually done is to change only the outward expression of those desires.

When you deal with the externals, what you are really doing is driving your soul farther outward from you spirit. The more your soul is focused on these outward things, the farther it is removed from its center and its resting place! The result of this type of self-denial is the opposite of what you sought . . .

If you dwell on the desires of your outward nature—paying attention to them—they, in turn, become more and more active. Instead of being subdued, they gain more power . . .

Then what is your hope? . . .

The only way to conquer your five senses is by turning your soul completely inward to your spirit, there to possess a present God. Your soul must turn all its attention and energies within, not without! Within to Christ, not without to your senses . . . Their life supply is cut off. They become powerless. . . .

Your main concern, therefore, is with the presence of Jesus Christ . . . You can be sure of this: The Christian who has faithfully abandoned himself to the Lord will soon discover that he also has laid hold of a God who will not rest until He has subdued everything! The Lord will put to death all that remains to be put to death in your life.

The blood of Christ flowing through your spirit-veins—the blood that contains the antidote to sin—that is the answer. Christ in you, your hope of glory! Turn your heart and your thoughts to Him and His powerful presence. You will find yourself being cleansed by His life.

REFLECT

You desire purity. You long to be free of your life-hindering flesh. Look to Him. He is the answer.

What temptations do you struggle against? Right now, surrender to the cleansing life. Ask Him to alert you to "crucifixion moments." Invite Him to train you in how to let temptation lead to purity.

Have you been to Jesus for the cleansing power?
Are you washed in the blood of the Lamb?
Are you fully trusting in His grace this hour?
Are you washed in the blood of the Lamb?

Lay aside the garments that are stained with sin,
And be washed in the blood of the Lamb;
There's a fountain flowing for the soul unclean,
O be washed in the blood of the Lamb!

Are you washed in the blood,
In the soul-cleansing blood of the Lamb?
Are your garments spotless? Are they white as snow?
Are your washed in the blood of the Lamb?

—"Are You Washed in the Blood?" by Elisha A. Hoffman

Write your thoughts.

_____

_____

_____

_____

_____

_____

_____

_____

_____

_____

_____

_____

_____

_____

_____

_____

_____

_____

THE WATER, THE SPIRIT, AND THE BLOOD

DAY ONE

"This is the one who came by water and blood—Jesus Christ. He did not come by water only, but by water and blood. And it is the Spirit who testifies, because the Spirit is the truth. For there are three that testify: the Spirit, the water and the blood; and the three are in agreement" (1 John 5:6–8).

List the three elements that are in agreement.

The blood has a partner: water. While blood speaks of forgiveness and inner cleansing, water speaks of an outward cleansing, a cleansing from defilement by the world.

Jesus came by water and blood. I believe John is specifically referring here to Jesus' baptism in the Jordan River (water) and His death on the cross (blood). These two events framed His ministry and His work as the last Adam. His water baptism launched His ministry. His death on the cross completed it.

BY WATER

Carefully read the account of Jesus' baptism in Luke 3:21–23; Mark 1:9–13; and Matthew 3:13–17.

What indications do you see that Jesus' baptism was a momentous event in the spiritual realm?

Which members of the Godhead were conspicuously present—made themselves known—at Jesus' baptism?

• the Father
• the Son
• the Spirit
• all of the above

What reason did Jesus give John for being baptized? (Matthew 3:15)

Jesus' water baptism has often been spoken of as an example to us—Jesus going through the motions in order to model the importance of baptism. It seems to me from Scripture's account that Jesus' baptism was far more important than that. It seems to me that it was a climactic moment, a pivotal event. The Spirit descended on Him in the form of a dove. The heavens opened and the Father spoke directly to the Son. All of heaven and the fullness of the Godhead were manifestly present at Jesus' baptism. You will see that, following Jesus' baptism, tremendous changes in His life and ministry occurred.

Jesus' baptism was not for cleansing from sin or for repentance. Rather, it was the formal priestly act that initiated His ministry. A form of baptism, known in Jewish practice as *micvah,* was part of a ceremony initiating a priest into his priestly service. It represented washing off or burying his old life and entering into his new life. Jesus said to John the Baptist, *"Let it be so now; it is proper for us to do this to fulfill all righteousness"* (Matthew 3:15). He was telling John, "It is fitting and appropriate for us to perform this ancient rite of *micvah.*" To put it in today's vernacular, I think Jesus was saying, "Let's do this by the book."

Jesus' baptism was the beginning of His active public ministry. His baptism was significant and it was public. He left behind His life of anonymity and obscurity and began His public ministry. He came by water.

BAPTIZED BY THE SPIRIT

The rite of water baptism is the shadow and the picture of true baptism: the baptism of the Spirit. The word "baptize" means "to be immersed in, to become one with."

At Jesus' baptism, the Holy Spirit descended upon Him. Being the Son of the Most High, born of the Holy Spirit, Jesus had always had the Holy Spirit *in* Him. He had always been full of the Holy Spirit. But it seems that, at His baptism, the Spirit anointed (covered, clothed) Him with a new dimension of power that would be manifested openly and outwardly in His speech and through His miracles. He was *"clothed with power from on high,"* which is how He described the anointing of the Holy Spirit upon His followers in Luke 24:49. The power that was *in* His life became also His outward garment. Let me repeat for clarification: Jesus already had the Holy Spirit in Him. He was filled with the Holy Spirit. At His baptism—the initiation into His public ministry—the Holy Spirit came *upon* Him anointing Him with power for performing miracles and speaking with authority (Acts 10:37–38).

Until the time of His baptism, there is no record of any miracle performed by Jesus. He seems not to have done anything to especially call attention to Himself. His friends and neighbors thought of Him as Joseph and Mary's son and were surprised to discover His growing fame.

After His baptism, a new dimension of power was upon Him. Luke reports that, following His baptism: *"Jesus, full of the Holy Spirit, returned from the Jordan and was led by the Spirit in the desert"* (Luke 4:1). There He was tempted by the devil. When the time of tempting was finished, Luke says, *"Jesus returned to Galilee in the power of the Spirit"* (Luke 4:14).

His return to Galilee clearly marked a new beginning in Jesus' life. *"News about him spread through the whole countryside. He taught in their synagogues, and everyone praised him"* (Luke 4:14–15). At this point we find His first recorded public message—He read in the synagogue a portion from the prophet Isaiah:

"The Spirit of the Lord is on me,
> *because he has anointed me*
> *to preach good news to the poor.*

He has sent me to proclaim freedom for the prisoners
and recovery of sight for the blind,
to release the oppressed,
to proclaim the year of the Lord's favor."
—Luke 4:18–19

"Today this scripture is fulfilled" (Luke 4:21). He proclaimed this very Scripture to be fulfilled in Him on that day. He was not saying that all the tasks had been accomplished, but that the anointing had occurred. That is the main action of the Scripture—the anointing. He was announcing His anointing by the Spirit and the launching of His ministry.

He was in His hometown, among people who had known Him all His life. Yet they seemed amazed by His new presence and power. *"All spoke well of him and were amazed at the gracious words that came from his lips. 'Isn't this Joseph's son?' they asked"* (Luke 4:22). Something was different about Jesus after His baptism. *"They were amazed at his teaching, because his message had authority"* (Luke 4:32).

He immersed Himself in water through baptism. When His mission reached its fulfillment, He poured out His blood. Water and blood.

At His baptism, the Spirit came upon Him with an anointing of power for ministry. At His crucifixion, He offered Himself *"through the eternal Spirit"* (Hebrews 9:14). The Spirit was actively involved in both His baptism and His crucifixion. *"For there are three that testify: the Spirit, the water and the blood; and the three are in agreement"* (1 John 5:7–8). The three converge on one truth. The three speak with one voice. The Spirit, the water, and the blood.

DAY TWO

SHADOW AND SUBSTANCE

Let's look at the shadows that were revealed in the old covenant, all meant to point to Christ and to the agreement of the water, the blood, and the Spirit.

THE HIGH PRIEST

Aaron, the first in the priestly line and a shadow of Christ, our high priest, entered his priesthood by water and blood. The Lord gave Moses these instructions: *"This is what you are to do to consecrate them, so they may serve me as priests"* (Exodus 29:1). Look at the shadow and the substance side-by-side. This is recorded in Exodus 29:4–11. These verses describe the ritual of initiation that would launch Aaron's ministry as priest. Following this ceremony, Aaron began his priestly service. You will see that Aaron came by water and blood.

Read Exodus 29:4–11. List below the four parts of the ritual of Aaron's priestly initiation. Then fill in the corresponding answers for Jesus.

Aaron	Jesus

Below are my answers. Aaron represents the shadow, the partial reality, and Jesus is the substance, the full realization of God's reality.

Aaron (shadow)	Jesus (substance)
Bring Aaron and his sons to the doorway of the tabernacle and wash them with water (publicly)	Jesus was baptized with water publicly
Place on Aaron the priestly garments to clothe him for his role	Jesus was "clothed with power from on high" to prepare him for His role
Pour the anointing oil on his head	In the synagogue, Jesus proclaimed His anointing
Slaughter the bull before the Lord	Shed His own blood on the altar

THE PRIESTLY TRIBE

The priestly tribe that descended from Aaron is a shadow of the church. Jesus, our high priest, is *"the firstborn among many brothers"* (Romans 8:29; Hebrews 12:23) and we are *"a holy priesthood"* (1 Peter 2:5, 9). In the tabernacle courtyard, the priests ("church") first encounter the blood, the inward purifying; then the water, the outer cleansing. Before the priests could enter the tabernacle to perform their duties, they had to come by water and blood.

In the outer courtyard of the tabernacle stood the altar of sacrifice, where sacrifices were slaughtered and their blood spilled. One other article stood in the outer courtyard: the laver of cleansing. Here the priests washed their hands and feet many times a day, washing away the world's dirt that clung to them. The priests could not enter the sanctuary of the tabernacle without coming through the blood and through the water.

The water and the blood agree. In other words, they are one. They are two parts of one whole. The inner cleansing and the outer washing. To put it in theological terms, the regeneration and the sanctification.

THE THREE WITNESSES

John says that there is a third testimony: the water, the blood, and the Spirit. The Spirit was active both in Jesus' baptism and in His crucifixion.

When, on the cross, Jesus' side was pierced, blood and water came out (John 19:34), the full picture of salvation: inner purity, outer cleansing. The Spirit of God bears witness with our spirits that we have been born of water and blood (Romans 8:16). The Spirit, the water, and the blood. The three stand in agreement, giving the same testimony, verifying one another.

DAY THREE

THE SHADOW: BLOOD SACRIFICES

Let's examine the blood sacrifices of the Old Testament. These are the shadow of the one eternal sacrifice. You will see that they foretold a two-fold role for the blood. The blood worked God-ward to reconcile and the blood worked man-ward to cleanse. You will also see that water and blood were partners. Where there was blood, there was water.

PASSOVER

In preparation for bringing the Israelites out of Egypt, where they had been slaves for four generations, God gave Moses the instructions they were to follow. On the last night in Egypt, God would set death loose to kill the firstborn of the land. The Israelites were to kill a spotless lamb and place its blood on the two door posts and on the lintel of their homes. They were not to leave their houses. They were not to leave the protection of the blood covering. God said to them, *"When I see the blood, I will pass over you"* (Exodus 12:13). The blood of an innocent lamb was shed in place of the life of their firstborn sons.

Read Exodus 12:1–13.

Write out the first sentence of verse 13. Circle or underline the phrase that tells how the blood works God-ward, and the phrase that tells how the blood works man-ward.

The blood of the Passover lamb played a two-fold role.

"On that same night I will pass through Egypt and strike down every firstborn—both men and animals—and I will bring judgment on all the gods of Egypt. I am the LORD. The blood will be a sign for you on the houses where you are; and when I see the blood, I will pass over you. No destructive plague will touch you when I strike Egypt" (Exodus 12:12–13).

The blood was a sign to the Israelites. It assured them of life. The blood of the Passover lamb provided life in the place of death. They were saved by the lamb's life, which was poured out for them.

The blood was a sign to God. It was the token and sign that the price had been paid. A life had been poured out. The Israelites were reconciled (the account was balanced; what they owed was paid) to God through the lamb's death.

The Israelites were about to leave one life behind and start a new life. They were leaving Egypt and slavery for Canaan and freedom. They were dying to their old life and being born again to their new life. Their transition was marked by water and blood.

When they left Egypt, they left through water, the Red Sea. Paul later recounts it this way: *"For I do not want you to be ignorant of the fact, brothers, that our forefathers were all under the cloud and that they all passed through the sea. They were all baptized into Moses in the cloud and in the sea"* (1 Corinthians 10:1–2). The transition from death to life was framed by blood and water. The water and blood agreed.

▼

Explain how the water and the blood agreed.

▲

PASSOVER SHADOWS

Although blood sacrifices had been offered since the time of Adam and Eve, this is the first official feast and ceremonial blood sacrifice God established. It lays the foundation for those that follow.

▼

Explain how you see these elements in the Passover story.

Innocent blood shed.

One life in place of another.

Blood works God-ward and blood works in lives of God's people.

Shedding of blood followed by waters of baptism.

DAY FOUR

CLEANSING OF THE LEPER

In the picture-language of the Old Testament, leprosy represents man's sinful condition—his Adam-life. Leprosy is a death in progress. Most often, when the Scripture is describing someone afflicted with leprosy, it says, "He is a leper" instead of saying, "He has leprosy." Why? Because our problem, before Christ, is not that we sin; rather our problem is that we *are sinners*. If the problem were that we sin, the answer would be to stop sinning. However, since we are sinners, we can't "not sin." The remedy for our leprous condition has to address the inner death that is manifesting itself in our sinful actions or flesh-based actions: "dead works." *"How much more will the blood of Christ, who through the eternal Spirit offered Himself without blemish to God, cleanse your conscience from dead works to serve the living God?"* (Hebrews 9:14 NASB).

To this day, there is no cure for leprosy. Yet, for the nation of Israel, there was a cleansing for leprosy. It is described in Leviticus 14. In the same way, there is no remedy for our sinful condition outside of the blood of Christ. In the cleansing of leprosy, not only were the outward manifestations, the flesh-eating sores, cleansed, but the person is no longer a leper. He no longer has the condition that produces the symptoms.

When you read Leviticus 14, where the ritual for cleansing a leper is recorded, you will notice that the person is initially referred to as "the leper." After the blood-cleansing, he is never again called "the leper," even though there are several more stages to complete the full "salvation" process.

Read Leviticus 14:1–20. Take note of the elements involved in the process and the steps that lead the leper from death to life. Write your thoughts below.

For the blood-cleansing of the leper, the priest went outside the camp, where the leper had been isolated for seven days. The high priest went to the leper. Our high priest went "outside the camp" in order to provide the blood-cleansing for us (Hebrews 13:11–12). He came to us in our sinful, death-filled condition.

The leper's blood cleansing required seven items. Seven is a significant number in Scripture. It represents God's completed work. God completed His work of creation in seven days. The seven items called for in the cleansing were: two clean birds, cedar wood, scarlet string, hyssop, an earthen vessel, and running water. The steps of the cleansing ritual are these:

1. Kill one bird in the earthen vessel over running water (v.5). The bird's blood and the running water are both caught in the earthen vessel. The earthen vessel represents the earth-body of Jesus, the Son of Man. Inside the earthen vessel was blood and water. The blood pictures the eternal life contained in an earthly form. The literal translation for "running water" is "living water." The running water pictured the Spirit in the earthly body of the Son of God.

This picture also depicts the eternal life and the living water in the earthen vessels—the bodies—of believers. The Spirit is living water in our innermost being (John 4:10; 7:38). *"We have this treasure in jars of clay to show that this all-surpassing power is from God and not from us"* (2 Corinthians 4:7).

2. The live bird and other elements are dipped in the blood of the slain bird (v. 6). They are not just lightly dipped. They are dunked under the blood and covered fully, soaked with it. Jewish literature says that the live bird was to be so sodden with the blood that it had to work to take flight. The live bird is the resurrection life that is made available to us because of the blood of Jesus shed from His earth-body. The live bird flies away after being covered with the blood. The live bird takes the blood into "the heavens."

One bird dies, the other lives. The two birds represent the two-fold role of the blood. One foreshadows that we are reconciled by His death—His life poured out; the other represents that we are saved by His life.

The cedar wood, scarlet string, and hyssop are dunked under the blood.

The cross has power in our lives because of His shed blood (cedar wood). The life is available to us because He shed His blood (scarlet string). Cleansing is ours because He shed His blood (hyssop).

3. The priest sprinkles the shed blood on the leper seven times (v.7). Seven is the number representing completed work. Jesus' earth-blood was sprinkled seven times, as we learned in Chapter One. Jesus' mission as the last Adam completed all that was necessary to reconcile us to the Father.

4. The leper is pronounced clean (v.7). From that point on he is not referred to as "the leper" again throughout the whole passage. We are pronounced "clean" because of Jesus' blood, which paid the price for our sins.

5. The live bird, dipped in blood, is set free (v.7). His death (earth-blood) and His life (Spirit-blood) work together for our complete salvation. The dead bird and the live bird: reconciled by His death and saved by His life.

6. The cleansed one is to wash himself in water. He is no longer a leper. He has been pronounced clean. Now he must wash away the elements of the world clinging to his flesh. He is baptized.

The Spirit and the water and the blood agree.

The cleansing ritual had a second tier. After seven days, the cleansed one returns to the priest. The elements of this ritual are these: two male lambs without defect, a yearling ewe lamb without defect, fine flour mixed with oil, a log of oil. The steps of the ritual are as follows:

1. One lamb is offered as a guilt offering or trespass offering (v. 12–13). This is the *asham* offering—the offering for the guilt of sinful acts or transgressions of law. The guilt offering's blood is shed for the forgiveness of our sins. Jesus is our guilt offering. The guilt offering is offered first. Jesus' earth-blood first paid for our sins, opening the way for all the other benefits of His blood to become active in our lives. The second tier process for lepers reminds us that even after we are pronounced clean, we must come into agreement with God (confess) over our wrong behaviors (sins) so that His blood can freely flow through us, cleansing us of unrighteousness (1 John 1:9).

2. The priest takes the blood of the guilt offering and places it on the person's right ear, right thumb, and big toe of his right foot (v. 14). The blood of the guilt offering covers every kind of sin. The whole person is covered with the blood. Just as in the tabernacle, every element was cleansed with blood, so God's living tabernacle is cleansed by blood. *"He sprinkled with the blood both the tabernacle and everything used in its ceremonies. In fact, the law requires that nearly everything be cleansed with blood"* (Hebrews 9:21–22).

3. The priest takes the oil and sprinkles it before the Lord seven times (v.16). While running water symbolizes the indwelling Spirit producing holiness, oil symbolizes the anointing of the Spirit for power. The oil is first sprinkled God-ward to remind us that like the blood, the power-anointing of the Spirit flows from the presence of the Father. The Spirit and the blood give the same testimony.

4. The priest takes the oil and places it *over the blood*: on the right ear, the right thumb, and the big toe of the right foot (v. 17). The oil is to be placed "on the blood of the guilt offering." The power-anointing of the Spirit can only be applied after the blood for the forgiveness of sins. Jesus shed His blood on the cross before the Spirit was poured out on the believers.

5. The remaining oil is poured over the cleansed one's head (v.18). This is the ritual for anointing a priest for his service (Psalm 133:2). It symbolizes that the power-anointing of the Spirit is for service.

6. The second male lamb is offered as a sin offering (v. 19). This is the sin offering, the *hattat* offering—the offering for our condition of sin, or our unrighteousness. He became sin for us (guilt offering) so that we could become righteousness in Him (sin offering). His blood flowing through our spirit-veins is cleansing us from unrighteousness. The blood had a two-fold role in the life of the cleansed leper: cleansing from *hattat* and forgiveness from *asham*.

7. The priest then sacrifices the ewe lamb as a burnt offering (vv. 19–20). The ewe (female) lamb is the bride of Christ, the church. The ewe lamb is to be unblemished, just as the church is to be *"a radiant church, without stain or wrinkle or any other blemish, but holy and blameless"* (Ephesians 5:27). She is to offer herself as a living sacrifice, pleasing to the Lord (Romans 12:1). The burnt offering represented the offering of the entire life to God. Like Christ, we offer our selves *"through the eternal spirit"* (Hebrews 9:14) In the Old Testament, a burnt offering is always described as "a pleasing aroma to the Lord." And *"we are to God the aroma of Christ"* (2 Corinthians 2:15).

8. The burnt offering of the ewe lamb is presented with the flour and oil mixture: the bread. The oil is what binds the flour into a bread-like mixture. The church is united by the Spirit (1 Corinthians 12:4–8). The Spirit and the blood agree.

DAY OF ATONEMENT

▽

Read Leviticus 16:3–34. We will focus on the atonement sacrifice for the whole nation, so especially take note of those details. Write your thoughts below.

△

The details of this yearly observance and sacrifice tell a multi-layered story, but for the purposes of this study, we will concentrate on the aspects of the ceremony that dealt with the sins of the people.

The Day of Atonement was once a year, every year. This was the only time the high priest entered into the Holy of Holies and sprinkled blood on the mercy seat. In the old covenant, the high priest had to first offer a sacrifice for his own sins. Only then could he offer the sacrifice for the sins of the people. This was true of the daily sin offerings, and on the Day of Atonement. In contrast, our high priest did not have to offer any sacrifice for His own sin (Hebrews 5:3). He was sinless.

"Unlike the other high priests, he does not need to offer sacrifices day after day, first for his own sins, and then for the sins of the people. He sacrificed for their sins once for all when he offered himself. For the law appoints as high priests men who are weak; but the oath, which came after the law, appointed the Son, who has been made perfect forever" (Hebrews 7:27–28).

In the symbols of the Day of Atonement, Jesus is both the atonement sacrifice on the cross and the high priest offering the sacrifice. When the high priest entered the Most Holy Place on the Day of Atonement, he did not wear his beautiful priestly robes, but instead was clothed humbly, in simple linen garments (Leviticus 16:4). When he comes out again, he changes from the linen garments into his priestly robes. Our eternal high priest was willing to humble Himself and dress Himself in humanity in order to make atonement for us. C. H. Spurgeon observes:

Oh! my soul, adore thy Jesus, who when he made atonement, humbled himself and wrapped around him a garb of thine inferior clay. Oh! angels, ye can understand what were the glories that he laid aside. Oh! thrones, and principalities, and powers, ye can tell what was the diadem with which he dispensed, and what, the robes he laid aside to wrap himself in earthly garbs. But, men, ye can scarce tell how glorious is your High Priest now, and ye can scarce tell how glorious he was before. But oh! adore him, for on that day it was the simple clean linen of his own body, of his own humanity, in which he made atonement for your sins.

—From a Sermon Delivered on Sabbath Morning, August 10, 1856, by the Rev. C. H. Spurgeon, New Park Street Chapel, Southwark

On the Day of Atonement (Leviticus 16), the sacrifice was as follows:

1. Aaron takes two male goats and presents them before the Lord (v.7). The two male goats represent the two-fold role of the blood.

2. Aaron is to cast lots for the goats. One will be the sin offering and the other will be the scapegoat (v.8). The literal translation of the word "scapegoat" is "goat of removal."

3. The scapegoat is to be presented alive before the Lord and sent into the wilderness alive (v.10). *"But the goat chosen by lot as the scapegoat shall be presented alive before the LORD to be used for making atonement by sending it into the desert as a scapegoat"* (Leviticus 16:10). Both goats, the one slaughtered and the one left alive, are making atonement, or reconciliation. One by its death, the other by its life.

4. The sin offering is slaughtered. Aaron takes its blood into the Holy of Holies and sprinkles it seven times on the mercy seat (v. 15). The number seven is symbolic of completed work. The blood works God-ward. It pays for sins. The people are reconciled to God through the death of the sin offering. The blood of goats and bulls is shadowing the reality that will be accomplished in the blood of Christ.

5. Aaron places his hands on the "goat of removal," confessing the peoples' sins (v.21). *"He is to lay both hands on the head of the live goat and confess over it all the wickedness and rebellion of the Israelites—all their sins—and put them on the goat's head"* (Leviticus 16:21). Laying hands on the sacrifice and confessing sins was part of every sin offering and guilt offering. In this ritual on the Day of Atonement, the high priest is acting as the representative of the people and speaking on their behalf. When laying hands on the sacrifice, the offerer was to lean all his or her weight on the animal, not just rest his hands on the animal's head. He was symbolically transferring the weight of his sin onto the animal. The animal was to bear the weight of the offerer's transgressions. So on this day, the high priest fully leaned into the goat, laying the burden of the people's sins on its head. How graphically this pictures our precious Savior: *"and the LORD has laid on him the iniquity of us all"* (Isaiah 53:6).

6. The "goat of removal' is then sent away alive (vv. 21–22). The scapegoat carries away the sins of the people through its life, not death. The life of the scapegoat is making atonement—reconciling God and man. The people are saved by the life of the scapegoat. Jesus' life continually "carries away" our sins.

7. Aaron bathes both before and after the sacrifices (vv. 4 and 24). The water (outer cleansing) and blood (inner cleansing) agree. They speak as one voice.

THE WHOLE PICTURE

The testimony of Scripture is consistent from beginning to end: our whole sin problem is remedied in the blood of Christ. We are reconciled by His death, but we are saved by His life. Not only did He pour out His blood for us, He also pours out His blood in us. The life—the eternal, overcoming, resurrection, cleansing life—is in you. God's everything is in you. The Kingdom's treasure is in you. How He loves you!

When I survey the wondrous cross,
On which the Prince of glory died,
My richest gain, I count but loss,
And pour contempt on all my pride.

Were the whole realm of nature mine,
That were a present far too small;
Love so amazing, so divine,
Demands my soul, my life, my all.

—"When I Survey the Wondrous Cross" by Isaac Watts

REFLECT

When the first innocent human blood was spilled, that of Abel, God said to his murderer: *"Listen! Your brother's blood cries out to me from the ground"* (Genesis 4:10). In the book of Hebrews we learn that Jesus' blood *"speaks a better word than the blood of Abel"* (Hebrews 12:24).

The blood of Abel cries out, "Justice!" The blood of Jesus cries out, "Mercy!"

The blood of Abel cries out, "Punish him!" The blood of Jesus cries out, "Let him go!"

The blood of Abel cries out, "Take his life in payment for mine!" The blood of Jesus cries out, "Take My life in payment for his!"

Do you hear the blood of Jesus crying out for you before the Father? Will you let His precious blood speak for you? Will you let His blood flow for you and through you?

Write your thoughts.

_____

_____

_____

_____

_____

_____

_____

_____

_____

_____

_____

_____

_____

_____

_____

THE HOPE OF GLORY

DAY ONE

In the beginning of this study I mentioned that the blood of Christ runs through every verse of the Bible, sometimes in the foreground, sometimes in the background. The whole message of salvation is wrapped up in the glorious blood of the Lamb.

When all the pieces come together and the whole picture is in view, the message of the blood of Christ is this: Christ in you. The mystery of the gospel that was hidden in the Old Covenant and revealed in the New Covenant is this: Christ in you.

This week, I want to take you back to the beginning and, with the understanding of the blood in place, trace the old, old story. I remember a hymn we used to sing when I was a child: "Tell me the story of Jesus, / Write on my heart every word; / Tell me the story most precious, / Sweetest that ever was heard" (Fanny J. Crosby, "Tell Me the Story of Jesus"). I want to tell you the story of Jesus. I want the finger of God to write on your heart every word.

THE GLORY OF GOD

Write out Romans 3:23.

Because of sin, all of us fall short of _____.

"For all have sinned and fall short of the glory of God." —Romans 3:23

Sin caused mankind to fall short of the *glory* of God. Not the expectations of God; not the standards of God; the *glory* of God. What is the glory of God? How did sin cause us to fall short of the glory?

The word "glory" is a multi-faceted word. In the Greek it is *doxa*; in Hebrew it is *kabowd*. It means "weightiness or value"—the weightier, the more valuable.

"Who among the gods is like you, O LORD?
> *Who is like you—*
>> *majestic in holiness,*
>> *awesome in glory,*
>> *working wonders?"*

—Exodus 15:11

It means "brightness or outshining."

"As he was praying, the appearance of his face changed, and his clothes became as bright as a flash of lightning . . . . Peter and his companions were very sleepy, but when they became fully awake, they saw his glory." —Luke 9:29, 32

It means "manifested presence"—the invisible put in visible form.

"For the Son of Man is going to come in his Father's glory." —Matthew 16:27

"The Son is the radiance of God's glory and the exact representation of his being." —Hebrews 1:3

"Then the cloud covered the Tent of Meeting, and the glory of the LORD filled the tabernacle. Moses could not enter the Tent of Meeting because the cloud had settled upon it, and the glory of the LORD filled the tabernacle." —Exodus 40:34–35

Let me pull all the layers together. Let's start with the word "outshining." If I were standing in front of you right now and you were seeing me, it would not be *me* you were seeing. You would be seeing the light rays that bounce off of me. You would be seeing my "outshining." The only way for you to know what I look like is for you to see the light rays that bounce off of me.

You can't see in the dark. In the dark, I would be invisible to you, even if I were present. So when you see my "outshining," you are seeing my "manifested presence," or my presence made visible. Even though I had been present all along, the light bouncing off of me would cause my presence to become visible. When I am revealed and my presence becomes visible, then my features emerge. My true value becomes obvious because I am on display. No longer am I covered by darkness (Psalm 97:2). Now, instead of guessing about me, you *see* me—I am revealed to you. You might say the light has made me known (John 1:18).

What does it mean that we have fallen short of the *glory* of God? To understand, we have to go all the way back to the beginning. In the creation account, the plural name for God, *Elohim*, is used. Throughout the account, the triune nature of God is emphasized. Notice the conversations that the Three-One God has with Himself.

*"Then God said, 'Let **us** make man in **our** image, in **our** likeness.' "* —Genesis 1:26

"And the Lord God said, 'The man has now become like one of us.' " —Genesis 3:22

The triune God is God the Father, God the Son, God the Spirit. When the Scripture refers to God or Jehovah, it is speaking of the Three-One. The triune God is Three acting as One; Three living and acting in such perfect harmony that they are One. In my book *Live a Praying Life*, I used the following illustration to describe the triune God.

Let me try to illustrate the oneness of the Father, the Son, and the Spirit in Their communication to you. Imagine that I have the most wonderful thoughts and that if you only knew my thoughts, your life would be changed forever. What would I have to do? I would have to translate my thoughts into words. Then my words would be the exact representation of my thoughts. My words would be my thoughts in a different form. The essence of my words and my thoughts would be exactly the same, but my thoughts would now be in the form of words.

It will take one more element for me to be able to get my thoughts across to you. It will take the breath of my mouth rushing over my vocal chords to form the voice that makes my words heard. My voice takes my words and makes them known to you.

Do you see how I speak *from* my thoughts, *through* my words, *by* my voice? Three actions in one.

Let my thoughts represent the Father, whose thoughts toward you are wonderful and precious according to Psalm 139:17–18; whose thoughts are higher than your thoughts according to Isaiah 55:8–9. The Father translated Himself into Word, according to John 1:1. Just as my thoughts are my words, so the Word was God. God the Father and God the Son are the same essence in different forms. The Thought was now in the form of Word (John 1:1–2, 14). The Word is the exact representation of the Thought (Hebrews 1:3). The Word makes the Thought known (John 1:18).

Now the third element: the Spirit. The Greek word *pneuma*, translated "Spirit," is also translated "breath." The Breath of God's mouth is a picture of the Holy Spirit throughout the Old Testament (Job 33:4; Ezekiel 37:9). Just as my breath creates the voice that delivers my words, the Spirit takes Jesus and makes Him known to you (John 16:15). *From* the Father, *through* the Son, *by* the Spirit.

The triune God is _____ acting in such perfect harmony that they are _____.

THE TRIUNE DESIGN

Elohim, the triune God, operates *from* the Father, *through* the Son, *by* the Spirit.

"And God [Father/ Divine Thought] *said* [Son/ Divine Word], *'Let there be light,' and there was light* [Spirit/ Divine Power]." —Genesis 1:3

*"Yet for us there is but one God, the Father, **from** whom all things came and for whom we live; and there is but one Lord, Jesus Christ, **through** whom all things came and **through** whom we live."* —1 Corinthians 8:6

*"Since we live **by** the Spirit."* —Galatians 5:25

Elohim created humankind (*adam*) in Their own image and likeness. *"Then God said, 'Let **us** make man in **our** image, in **our** likeness'"* (Genesis 1:26). The triune God created a **triune being**. He created *adam* with spirit, soul, body. *"The LORD God formed the man from the dust of the ground* (body) *and breathed into his nostrils the breath of life* (spirit), *and the man became a living being* (soul)" (Genesis 2:7).

Humans were designed to be the "glory" of God. They were created to operate according to the Triune Design: *from* the spirit, *through* the soul, *by* the body. The spirit was to be the command-center of the soul; the soul was the command-center of the body.

Elohim's intention in creating Adam and Eve was to point to them and say, "Do you want to know what I look like? Look at him. Look at her. They are My outshining." He wanted mankind to be able to say, "If you've seen me, you've seen the Father." Mankind was intended to be the glory of God.

Humans were designed so that the body, soul, and spirit were to operate in perfect harmony. Spirit, soul, and body were to operate in such perfect harmony that they would be one. Humans were to be the glory—the outshining, the manifested presence—of Elohim. His purpose for mankind was to make Him known, to shine the spotlight on Him.

SIN DISRUPTED THE TRIUNE DESIGN

The Deceiver appealed to the human soul. The soul (mind, will, emotions) responded to the appeal and acted through the body. Now the harmony was disrupted. The human soul acted as its own master rather than as the vehicle through which the spirit operated. With the entrance of sin, not only did mankind come into conflict with God, but he also came into conflict with himself. His spirit, soul, and body were out of sync. Paul describes this state of death in Romans 7. Mankind sinned and so fell short of the *glory* of God.

State your understanding of what it means to fall short of the glory of God.

DAY TWO

GOD'S PLAN FOR RESTORING HIS GLORY

From the beginning, God had a plan for how He would restore His glory. The plan goes like this: *"Christ **in you**, the hope of glory"* (Colossians 1:27).

The whole Bible is about Christ in you. Do you see that the central theme of Scripture—the blood of Christ—is about *Christ in you*? Once you understand Christ in you, you will understand the whole Bible.

Read Colossians 1:25–28.

"I have become its (the church's) *servant by the commission God gave me to present to you the word of God in its fullness—the mystery that has been kept hidden for ages and generations, but is now disclosed to the saints. To them God has chosen to make known among the Gentiles the glorious riches of this mystery, which is Christ in you, the hope of glory."*

What is Paul's commission?

Why had the word of God not previously been presented in its fullness?

What is the mystery that had previously been hidden, but is now disclosed? What is "the word of God in its fullness"?

Paul's commission is "to present the word of God in its fullness." Until then, the message was not fully presented. It had been kept hidden. The shadows could be seen, but not the substance. It was a mystery. But now, says Paul, that which had been hidden is revealed. It is brought out into the open and made plain. The fullness of the message can now be seen. And what is that message? What is the fullness of the Word of God? It can all be summed up in one phrase: Christ in you, the hope of glory.

Paul makes the same point in his letter to the Romans, but adds a key crucial to our understanding of the gospel.

"Now to him who is able to establish you by my gospel and the proclamation of Jesus Christ, according to the revelation of the mystery hidden for long ages past, but now revealed and made known through the prophetic writings by the command of the eternal God, so that all nations might believe and obey him—to the only wise God be glory forever through Jesus Christ! Amen." —Romans 16:25–27

Paul refers to "my gospel and the proclamation of (about) Jesus Christ." This announcement about Jesus Christ had been "hidden for long ages past." Now, Paul says, this hidden mystery is "revealed and made known." We already know that the mystery is "Christ in you, the hope of glory."

Where was the mystery hidden? In the prophetic writings—the Old Testament. How is the mystery being revealed? From the prophetic writings by the command of the eternal God. The whole Old Testament is about *Christ in you.*

The message of the Old Testament had always been "Christ in you," but only since the Spirit of Christ has come to indwell believers has the message been made plain and brought out into the open.

THE TRIUNE DWELLING PLACE

God painted a picture of the mystery—of His eternal plan for restoring His glory to His people—when He gave Moses instructions to build the tabernacle. The tabernacle was a portable worship center that the Israelites moved with them from encampment to encampment as they journeyed through the desert. *Tabernacle* means "dwelling place." The verb form of the word for tabernacle means "to dwell."

"Then have them make a sanctuary for me, and I will dwell (tabernacle) *among them. Make this tabernacle* (dwelling place) *and all its furnishings exactly like the pattern I will show you. . . . See that you make them according to the pattern shown you on the mountain."* —Exodus 25:8–9, 40

God says that in the tabernacle, He will dwell among His people. The word *among* is from a root that literally means "to sever." By implication, the word means to be the center, to be inside. Do you see what He is saying? The tabernacle would be His dwelling place "inside" His people. The tribes were to place their tents around the tabernacle so that the dwelling place was "inside" them.

He made it clear that He was giving Moses instructions that would paint a time-bound picture of an eternal reality. He was creating a visual of the eternal reality: Christ in you, the hope of glory.

"They serve at a sanctuary that is a copy and shadow of what is in heaven. This is why Moses was warned when he was about to build the tabernacle: 'See to it that you make everything according to the pattern shown you on the mountain.'"
—Hebrews 8:5

*"Have them make a sanctuary for me, and **I will dwell** (tabernacle) **among them.**"*
—Exodus 25:8

*"The Word became flesh and **made his dwelling** (tabernacled) **among us**. We have seen his glory, the glory of the One and Only, who came from the Father, full of grace and truth."* —John 1:14

*"So that Christ may **dwell** (tabernacle) **in your hearts** through faith."*
—Ephesians 3:17

TRIUNE STRUCTURE

The tabernacle was a triune dwelling place. The tabernacle was made up of the Holy of Holies, the Holy Place (sanctuary), and the Outer Courtyard.

The Holy of Holies is a picture of our spirit, where God takes up residence. The Holy Place, the sanctuary, is a picture of our soul. The sanctuary contains the candlestick (mind), the bread of the presence (will), and altar of incense (emotions). The outer courtyard is a picture of our bodies.

The tabernacle is a 2-layered picture.

• As I move from the outside toward the inside, I see a picture of *what* Christ did *for* me.

• As I move from the inside to the outside, I see a picture of *who* Christ is *in* me.

Many books and very fine studies have been written detailing the symbolism of the tabernacle as it pictures what Christ did for you. Fewer emphasize the second layer: who Christ is in you. For this study, we will briefly touch on the tabernacle picture. We will spend the most time on the Mercy Seat, where the precious blood of the Lamb flows day and night.

ECHOES OF CREATION

Notice the language similarities between the account of Elohim in creation, crowned by His creation of mankind, and Moses building the tabernacle. This hints at the symbolic ties between the two. The account of Moses' work on the tabernacle is an echo of Elohim's work in the creation of humans. The tabernacle was a picture of God's purposed design for mankind.

Creation: *"Thus the heavens and the earth were completed in all their vast array"* (Genesis 2:1).
Tabernacle: *"So all the work on the tabernacle, the Tent of Meeting, was completed"* (Exodus 39:32).

Creation: *"God saw all that he had made, and it was very good"* (Genesis 1:31).
Tabernacle: *"Moses inspected the work and saw that they had done it just as the LORD had commanded"* (Exodus 39:43).

Creation: *"God had finished the work he had been doing"* (Genesis 2:2).
Tabernacle: *"And so Moses finished the work"* (Exodus 40:33).

Creation: *"And God blessed the seventh day"* (Genesis 2:3).
Tabernacle: *"So Moses blessed them"* (Exodus 39:43).

TABERNACLE SHADOWS

Outer Courtyard/ Body		
Furniture	**What Christ did for you**	**Who Christ is in you**
Altar of Sacrifice	*"How much more, then, will the blood of Christ, who through the eternal Spirit* **offered himself unblemished to God***, cleanse our consciences from acts that lead to death, so that we may serve the living God!"* (Hebrews 9:14). *"For what I received I passed on to you as of first importance: that* **Christ died for our sins** *according to the Scriptures"* (1 Corinthians 15:3).	*"We always carry around* **in our body** *the death of Jesus, so that the life of Jesus may also be revealed in our body"* (2 Corinthians 4:10). *"Therefore, I urge you, brothers, in view of God's mercy, to* **offer your bodies as living sacrifices***, holy and pleasing to God—this is your spiritual act of worship"* (Romans 12:1).
Laver of Cleansing	*"Who* **gave himself for us** *to redeem us from all wickedness and* **to purify** *for himself a people that are his very own, eager to do what is good"* (Titus 2:14). *"After* **he had provided purification for sins***, he sat down at the right hand of the Majesty in heaven"* (Hebrews 1:3).	*"The blood of Jesus, his Son ,* **purifies*** *us from all sin"* (1 John 1:7). *"How much more, then, will the blood of Christ, who through the eternal Spirit* **offered himself unblemished to God***, cleanse our consciences from acts that lead to death, so that we may serve the living God!"* (Hebrews 9:14). *By flowing through our spirit-veins.

Sanctuary/Soul		
Furniture	**What Christ did for you**	**Who Christ is in you**
Golden Candlestick (mind)	"While I am in the world, **I am the light** of the world" (John 9:5). "The people living in darkness have seen a great light; on those living in the land of the shadow of death a light has dawned" (Matthew 4:16).	"**You are the light** of the world ... let **your light** shine before men, that they may see your good deeds and praise your Father in heaven" (Matthew 5:14, 16). "I pray also that the eyes of your heart may be **enlightened** in order that you may **know***" (Ephesians 1:18). *The Light of Christ enlightens your understanding.
Bread of the Presence (will)	"'For the bread of God is he who comes down from heaven and gives life to the world.' . . . Then Jesus declared, '**I am the bread of life**. He who comes to me will never go hungry, and he who believes in me will never be thirsty'" (John 6:33, 35)	"I am the living bread that came down from heaven. **If anyone eats of this bread***, he will live forever. This bread is my flesh, which I will give for the life of the world" (John 6:51). "While they were eating, Jesus took **bread**, gave thanks and broke it, and gave it to his disciples, saying, '**Take and eat***; this is my body'" (Matthew 26:26) *As His life indwells you, He begins to transform your desires and your will. "For it is God who works **in you** to will . . . his good pleasure" (Philippians 2:13). What is His good pleasure? "'My food,' said Jesus, 'is to do the will of him who sent me and to finish his work'" (John 4:34). As you feast on the Bread of Life, your food is to do the will of Him who sent you.
Altar of Incense* (emotions) *Incense is connected to intercession, e.g., "May my prayer be set before you like incense" (Psalm 141:2).	"Christ Jesus, who died—more than that, who was raised to life—is at the right hand of God and **is also interceding for us**" (Romans 8:34–35). "Therefore he is able to save completely those who come to God through him, because he always **lives to intercede for them**" (Hebrews 7:25).	"Because you are sons, God sent the Spirit of his Son **into our hearts***, the Spirit who calls out, 'Abba, Father'" (Galatians 4:6). "God has poured out **his love** into **our hearts*** by the Holy Spirit, whom he has given us" (Romans 5:5). *The love that compels Him to continual intercession is poured into us; His loving intercession is expressed through our prayers.

Tomorrow we will look at the third part of the triune dwelling place.

The third part of the triune design is the Holy of Holies, a picture of our spirit. Here we have the Ark of the Covenant, which is covered by the Mercy Seat.

When Jesus, our precious High Priest, took His eternal, overcoming life into the Holy of Holies, He *became* the Mercy Seat. The Ark of the Covenant and its covering Mercy Seat in the earth-tabernacle is a wonderful picture of Christ in you.

The Ark of the Covenant was made of Acacia wood—representing Jesus' sinless humanity. It was covered outside and lined inside with pure gold—representing Jesus' perfect divinity.

His humanity is sandwiched between the two layers of gold, which tells us that He was always God. He was in the beginning with God (John 1:1–2). All things were created by Him and before Him and He is before all things (Colossians 1:17). Then, after He completed His job as the last Adam, He returned to His full divinity. He returned to the glory He had in the beginning (John 17:5).

The Ark of the Covenant contained three items: the tablets of the Law, Aaron's rod that budded even though it was dead, and a golden container of manna. These three items represent the Triune God. The tablets of the Law represent the Father. Aaron's rod represents the Spirit. Aaron's rod pictures resurrection—life that comes out of death. The Spirit is the One who raised Jesus from the dead and is now living in us (Romans 8:11). The manna represents the Son (John 6:32–33).

The fullness of the Godhead was in the Ark of the Covenant. *"For in Christ all the fullness of the Deity lives in bodily form"* (Colossians 2:9). *"For God was pleased to have all his fullness dwell in him"* (Colossians 1:19).

The Ark of the Covenant was covered with the Mercy Seat. The Mercy Seat was made of pure gold beaten into the size and shape that would exactly cover the Ark of the Covenant. There is much beautiful symbolism in the details of the Mercy Seat, but I want to concentrate on this: on the Day of Atonement, the blood of the atonement sacrifice was sprinkled on the Mercy Seat. The Mercy Seat, like the body of Jesus on the cross, was covered with nothing but the blood. All the other parts of the sacrifice were offered outside the Holy of Holies. Only the blood was applied the Mercy Seat.

The High Priest did not speak when he went into the Holy of Holies with the blood of atonement sacrifice. The blood on the Mercy Seat said it all. The blood of Jesus speaks for us (Hebrews 12:24).

It was over the Mercy Seat, after the blood had been sprinkled, that the *Shekinah* presence of God appeared. Only at the Mercy Seat did heaven and earth meet, and that meeting was only in the blood. The priest himself did not touch the Mercy Seat. He dipped his finger into the blood and sprinkled the blood.

The Ark of the Covenant covered by the Mercy Seat was the one and only place that the presence of God dwelled. Access was restricted. Only the High Priest could enter in, and he only once a year and only with blood. Earth could not touch heaven except through the blood. So strict was this prohibition that any

Israelite who touched the Ark of the Covenant for any reason died immediately.

In Jesus, heaven and earth met. The Word became flesh. In His blood, His God-life was exposed to the sin-disease. He was tempted in every point like we are. In His blood, He created the antidote to sin and death. The power of heaven came into the circumstances of earth. God met man in the person of Jesus.

When our Great High Priest went into the heavenly tabernacle with His own blood, He had become the reality that the Mercy Seat shadowed. He had *become* the source of eternal salvation.

▼

Recap how the mystery of Christ in you has always been hidden in the Old Testament.

Triune God created man, a _____ being, in His image, created to be His _____. _____ caused man to fall short of the glory of God.

From the beginning, God had a plan for how to restore His _____. He kept the reality of the plan hidden for ages and generations, to be revealed in Christ. The plan was "_____" (Colossians 1:27).

God created a picture of the eternal plan by instructing Moses to build for Him a _____ dwelling place, where He would dwell _____ His people.

▲

DAY FIVE

THE FULLNESS OF GOD IN CHRIST

Jesus, during His days as a man, claimed to be the Temple (a permanent structure based on the tabernacle). *"Jesus answered them, 'Destroy this temple, and I will raise it again in three days.' . . . But the temple he had spoken of was his body"* (John 2:19, 21). What made His body the Temple? The Father lived in Him. *"It is the Father, living in me, who is doing his work"* (John 14:10). He was the dwelling place of God. He was the glory—the outshining, the manifested presence—of God. His body was the container of life. "As the Father has life in himself, so he has given me to have life in myself" (John 5:26).

We have already seen that the fullness of the Godhead tabernacled in Jesus: *"For in Christ all the fullness of the Deity lives in bodily form"* (Colossians 2:9). *"For God was pleased to have all his fullness dwell in him"* (Colossians 1:19). Look with me for what it means to you and me that the fullness of God is in Jesus. *"For God was pleased to have all his fullness dwell in him, and through him to reconcile to himself all things, whether things on earth or things in heaven, by making peace through his blood, shed on the cross."* —Colossians 1:19–20

Now earth can touch heaven! Because God tabernacled in the body of Jesus, and because the life came to earth, heaven and earth have been brought together at the Mercy Seat—our lovely, precious Jesus. He brings heaven into earth and earth into heaven. He stands in the gap between heaven and earth.

The life that was in His earth-body, the fullness that is in Him, is being transfused into us. *"For in Christ all the fullness of the Deity lives in bodily form,* ***and you have been given fullness in Christ"*** (Colossians 2:9–10).

A HOUSE OF GLORY

You are the tabernacle. You are the dwelling place. You are the place where He displays His glory. You are the place where His glory is "at home."

"Don't you know that you yourselves are God's temple and that God's Spirit lives in you? If anyone destroys God's temple, God will destroy him; for God's temple is sacred, and you are that temple." —1 Corinthians 3:16–17

"Do you not know that your body is a temple of the Holy Spirit, who is in you, whom you have received from God?" —1 Corinthians 6:19

"For we are the temple of the living God." —2 Corinthians 6:16

When Jesus lived as a man on earth, His body was the Temple. Now your body is the Temple. You are His house. He created you to be His dwelling place.

From the moment He takes up residence in you—when He comes to inhabit His Holy of Holies—He begins a renovation project. He begins to restore your soul.

When He takes His place in you, your spirit is immediately made perfect and whole. But your soul is filled with debris. He begins to clean out all the flesh-patterns and all the sin-habits. He is purifying you. His goal is not only to cleanse you of sin, but also to *fill you with Himself.*

He promises this: *" 'I will fill this house with glory,' says the LORD Almighty. . . . 'The glory of this present house will be greater than the glory of the former house,' says the LORD Almighty. 'And in this place I will grant peace,' declares the LORD Almighty"* (Haggai 2:7, 9).

Write out Haggai 2:9.

What is God speaking directly to your heart from these words?

Can you imagine how breathtakingly beautiful the Temple was? Yet, you—Christ in you—are even more stunning. You are a design that the Temple and the tabernacle could only hint at. You are filled with the glory—the presence of Christ.

When your soul is cleansed of flesh, then God says, "In this place I will grant peace." Do you remember the original triune design? Spirit, soul, and body were to operate in such perfect harmony that they would be one. That is the peace that Elohim is granting—peace within. Spirit, soul, and body no longer at odds.

Elohim wants to point to you and say, "If you've seen her—if you've seen him—then you've seen Me."

A HOUSE OF PRAYER

He says of His tabernacle: "My house shall be called a house of prayer." He is making you a house of prayer. He is creating in you an environment where there is a continual interaction between heaven and earth. He is doing His work from the inside. Christ in you, the hope of glory.

REFLECT

You must decrease and He must increase. Let your littleness be absorbed by His greatness. Let your weakness be swept away by His strength. Let your failure, your fear, your struggles, your bitterness . . . let it all be flushed out by the powerful flow of His life in you. Take your eyes off yourself. Fix your eyes on Him. Hide yourself in Him. Worship with the words of this classic hymn.

Rock of Ages, cleft for me,
Let me hide myself in Thee;
Let the water and the blood,
From Thy wounded side which flowed,
Be of sin the double cure,
Save from wrath and make me pure.

Not the labors of my hands
Can fulfill Thy law's demands;
These for sin could not atone;
Thou must save, and Thou alone:

In my hand no price I bring,
Simply to Thy cross I cling.

While I draw this fleeting breath,
When mine eyes shall close in death,
When I rise to worlds unknown,
And behold Thee on Thy throne,
Rock of Ages, cleft for me,
Let me hide myself in Thee.

—"Rock of Ages, Cleft for Me" by Augustus M. Toplady

What does it mean to you to be a house of His glory? Write out your thoughts.

_____

_____

_____

_____

_____

_____

_____

_____

_____

_____

_____

_____

THE BREAD
AND THE WINE

DAY ONE

As you bring your study to a close, this week's material is designed to let you review the concepts in ways that will make them personal for you, not just theoretical. This week's material is more devotional in nature than the format of the previous weeks has been.

This week, in light of new and deeper understanding, I hope that you will behold the Lamb.

▼

"Remember that at that time you were separate from Christ, excluded from citizenship in Israel and foreigners to the covenants of the promise, without hope and without God in the world. But now in Christ Jesus you who once were far away have been brought near through the blood of Christ." —Ephesians 2:12–13

Take some time to consider what it would mean to you, right now, in your right-now circumstances, to be "separate from Christ." Describe your thoughts.

Describe what difference it makes in your life that you have been brought into oneness with God (Father, Son, and Spirit) through the blood of Christ.

Make this your prayer: *Jesus! How can I find words to tell You how awed I am that You would give Yourself as my bringing-near offering! I can enter boldly into the Holy of Holies because of Your blood in me. I fall on my face and am left speechless by the wonder of it all. I, who was once far away, have been brought near by the blood of Christ!*

Create an acrostic of the word "near" as it speaks of the blood. Don't feel that it has to form a coherent sentence. Just list words that begin with the letters n-e-a-r and that relate to your understanding of the blood. It could be sentences or phrases.

N

E

A

R

DAY TWO

"And he took bread, gave thanks and broke it, and gave it to them, saying, 'This is my body given for you; do this in remembrance of me.'" —Luke 22:19

Jesus uses a word that is translated here "given" that means delivered up, smitten, laid down, handed over. As He broke the bread, He used the moment to say, "This—this broken bread—*this* is My body."

Matthew reports it this way: *"While they were eating, Jesus took bread, gave thanks and broke it, and gave it to the disciples, saying, 'Take and eat; this is my body'"* (Matthew 26:26).

His earthly blood was part of His earthly body. It was in His body that He overcame the power of sin, that He built up the antibodies against sin-death. It was in His body that He became sin for you, fought your battles, won your victories. He carried your sin in His body on the tree.

▼

Put yourself at that table. In that moment, the disciples did not recognize its significance, but you do. Through sanctified imagination, be present there; be part of the event. As He offers you the broken bread, both you and He know what it shadows.

Hear Him say your name. He calls you by name and looks you in the eye as He says, "This is My body which is broken *for you*." What do you say back to Him? Write it out.

As you take the bread from His hand and eat it, you know that you are partaking of Eternal Life. In His body, He reconciled you by His death.

Create an acrostic for "death" in light of your new understanding.

D

E

A

T

H

▲

DAY THREE

"In the same way, after the supper he took the cup, saying, 'This cup is the new covenant in my blood, which is poured out for you.'" —Luke 22:20

Recall that when Jesus told His disciples that His blood would be "poured out" for them, it was a direct echo from the old covenant sacrificial system when all the blood from the blood sacrifice was dashed against the base of the altar. But recall also that the eternal blood, of which the earth blood was a shadow, was all poured

out in the heavenly tabernacle for you. Salvation is in His blood, and His blood is in you. You are saved by His life.

Through sanctified imagination, once again be present at the table, knowing what you know. Let Him offer you the cup of salvation. Take it from His hand. In the earth-time context at the moment in history, His hands were not yet pierced. But you see the eternal reality. As you take the cup from His hands, you see His blood flowing freely for you.

As He speaks your name and offers you the cup of the new covenant in His blood, how do you respond?

Create an acrostic for the word "life" in light of what you now understand.

L

I

F

E

DAY FOUR

"If we confess our sins, he is faithful and just and will forgive us our sins and purify us from all unrighteousness." — 1 John 1:9

We have looked at this verse of Scripture often during this study. Yet there is one more truth hidden here that we have not examined. What is John referencing when he says that God will forgive us and cleanse us because He is faithful and just? *Faithful* to what? *Just* in what way?

Can you stand one more chart? It helps me to organize information so that it speaks visually. So indulge me one last time.

Problem	Solution	Promise	Character of God
Sins we commit	Reconciled by His death	Forgive our sins	Faithful
Root of unrighteousness	Saved by His life	Purify us from all unrighteousness	Just

He is faithful to the covenant. *Faithful* means trustworthy, a keeper of His word. When God made an everlasting covenant with Abraham and Abraham's offspring, He put Abraham into a deep sleep. While Abraham slept, God performed the covenant rituals Himself. Typically, a covenant is between two parties. Each makes certain promises, then the covenant is sealed by the shedding of blood. However, in this case, recorded in Genesis 15:12–21, God Himself, in the form of a smoking firepot and a burning torch, performed the whole covenant ritual— while Abraham slept.

The writer of Hebrews explained it this way: *"When God made his promise to Abraham, since there was no one greater for him to swear by, he swore by himself, saying, 'I will surely bless you and give you many descendants'"* (Hebrews 6:13–14). God promised Himself that He would keep both sides of the covenant that He made with Abraham. He shed His own blood to atone for the sins of Abraham's offspring, and He is faithful to the covenant.

The conditions have been met that provide for our forgiveness. When we come into agreement with Him about our sins, He is faithful to the covenant.

He is *just*. In other words, He is fair; He balances the scales. Having accomplished that part of the covenant agreement that provides for the payment of our debt, He now completes the covenant by making us able, by His own indwelling life, to be cleansed from the unrighteousness that causes us to sin. Andrew Murray explains it this way in his book *The Two Covenants*:

This passage brings into view that which is the distinctive blessing of the New Covenant. In working out our salvation God bestowed upon us two wonderful gifts. We read, "*God sent forth His Son*, that He might redeem them that were under the law, that we might receive the adoption of sons. And because we are sons, *God sent forth the Spirit of His Son* into your hearts crying, Abba, Father." Here we have the two parts of God's work in salvation. The one, the more objective, what He did that we might become His children—He sent forth His Son. The second, the more subjective, what He did that we might live like His children: He sent forth the Spirit of His Son into our hearts. In the former we have the external manifestation of the work of redemption; in the other, its inward appropriation; the former for the sake of the latter. These two halves form the great whole and cannot be separated.
—From *The Two Covenants*, by Andrew Murray

Do you see? He is faithful—He will forgive your sins; He is just—He will purify you from all unrighteousness.

When you recognize and agree with God about the roots of unrighteousness that produce sin-fruit in your life, whose problem does it immediately become? Upon whose power does the answer depend?

What does it mean to you at this moment in your life that He is faithful and just?

Create an acrostic for the word "pure" in light of your understanding of the blood.

P

U

R

E

DAY FIVE

Reflect on the study. If you have made it all the way to the last day of the last week, then you have invested much in unlocking the secrets of the blood of Christ. I know that it will not be wasted effort. I know that your understanding will continue to grow and you will see the blood every time you open your Bible.

What concept was most life-altering for you?

In what way are you more grateful than ever for your salvation?

What will change about the way you live your life because of your new under-standing of the blood of Christ?

"For God was pleased to have all his fullness dwell in him, and through him to reconcile to himself all things, whether things on earth or things in heaven, by making peace through his blood, shed on the cross." —Colossians 1:19–20

Today, I want to do the acrostic for you.

P artaking of our humanity, the Son of God

E mptied Himself

A nd taking upon Himself the form of a man

C ame from heaven to earth to bring

E ternal Life

OPTIONAL CLOSING WORSHIP EXPERIENCE

This is a plan for a worship experience that will bring your study to a close. If you have been doing the study alone, plan a private worship experience for yourself.

If you are not in charge of planning and leading the worship experience, you do not need to read further. Just arrive at your meeting place right on time this week, prepared to worship the Lamb.

Here is a list of articles you might use in your worship experience. Gather the things on the list you may want to use.

Candles
Potpourri
Electric water pump/ fountain
Hymn books or song sheets
CD player, tape player, or someone to play piano softly in the background
A small piece of paper for each participant
Loaf of bread
Grape juice
Communion cups

As you plan for your worship, plan an experience that will engage all the senses. Keep each element simple. For example, as you plan for aroma, remember that some people may not enjoy the aroma, and some people are allergic to strong scents. So have aroma, but keep it light. I listed as a suggestion an electric water fountain because the gentle sound of flowing water is very soothing, but you may prefer to have quiet music playing in the background instead.

Plan for music during your experience. Shape your plan to fit your group. In writing this study, I have come to love the old, classic hymns about the blood of Christ. I hope that the familiar words have taken on fresh meaning. Maybe you would plan to use the hymns that have been part of each week's lesson. You might plan for someone to lead the group in song and/ or to sing a solo. You might plan to reproduce the lyrics to all songs you will sing on a song sheet for each participant.

In the back of this book, you will find sheet music with vocal and piano parts for a song called "The Spirit's Quiet Whisper." This will be a good song to use both to open and close the worship experience. You can order a CD with the song "The Spirit's Quiet Whisper" sung by Roxanne Lingle. The CD also contains an instrumental track so you can use it to accompany the song. Order the CD from The Praying Life Foundation at www.prayinglife.org or by calling 888-844-6647.

As part of this worship experience, I am suggesting a communion-like activity using bread and grape juice. Be sure that you respect any denominational regulations so that your church leadership would not feel offended. Personally, I think of it as part of a worship experience, but that you are not offering it as an official sacrament of the church. If, however, your pastor or other church staff feel differently about it, you will certainly want to accommodate those concerns.

Depending on the size of your group, ask several people to be small group leaders. Their primary job will be to serve the communion elements to their group members. If your group is small, you may be one group. In that case, still have a person or two who will serve the elements. The experience of being served will be important. Don't have group members come to the serving table and get their own elements. Instead, plan to serve them.

BEFORE ATTENDEES ARRIVE:

• Prepare the room using the elements you have chosen to provide a worship experience that engages all the senses.

• Arrange the room's seating in small circles of no more than 5 chairs in each group.

• Place a song sheet and the small slip of paper on each chair.

• Create a "serving table" with the loaf of bread, the grape juice, and the communion cups.

• Pray over each chair for the person who will sit in that place. Ask the Lord to reveal Himself and speak in personal ways to that person.

AS ATTENDEES ARRIVE:

• Encourage them to enter worshipfully, take a seat, and sit quietly in the Lord's presence.

• Have each group leader already seated in his or her grouping of chairs.

DURING THE WORSHIP EXPERIENCE:

• Open with the song "The Spirit's Quiet Whisper." You might have it as a solo, or teach it to the group and then sing it worshipfully, or play the recording.

• Invite people to share testimonies about how God has taught them and changed them through the study of the blood of the Lamb. Some might want to share a Scripture that has taken on new meaning. Others might want to share a truth that was transforming to their lives. According to your group's size and personality, do this in small groups or as a large group.

• Have a worship time, using Scripture and music. I suggest that you go through the study and choose defining Scriptures for each topic, then intersperse reading of Scripture with worshipful songs. For example:

1. Assign people to read the following verses to illuminate "The Life" —John 1:4; 1 John 5:12; 1 John 1:9.

2. Sing the hymn "Nothing But the Blood," or use it as a responsive reading, with the group reading "nothing but the blood of Jesus" in response to a leader reading the other lines. Then sing the chorus in unison.

3. Plan something along those lines to cover each week of the study. Let the Scripture reading and the worshipful singing flow together into a seamless experience.

4. Lead from the worship time into a reverent time of sharing in the elements of the communion. This is likely to be a very moving part of your worship experience. The leader should go to the serving table. Here is a suggested script for serving the communion elements. Have worshipful music playing softly in the background.

SUGGESTED SCRIPT FOR COMMUNION

Leader: As we use these earthly pictures—bread and juice—to stand for spiritual reality, let us come to this moment with awe and reverence. Let the eyes of your heart be focused on the face of Jesus.

Leader: I remind you that we have been reconciled to the Father by the death of the Lord Jesus, and we are being saved by the Life of the Lord Jesus. Let this truth settle down and make a home for itself in your heart.

Leader: We turn first to His body, which was broken for us. (*Break the loaf as you say this.*) As we, in a moment, partake of the bread, we are reminded that as He hung on the cross, He was covered by nothing but the blood. That as the blood poured out from His body, it covered my sins. In Him, my sins were covered by nothing but the blood. As we think upon His broken body, we are reminded that we are reconciled by His death.

Leader: As you continue to worship in the inner sanctuary of your own soul—as you gaze upon that old, rugged cross, so despised by the world, it has a wondrous attraction for you—your group leader will bring the bread to serve you. As you hold it in your hand until the appropriate time, let it remind you of His precious body.

(*Group leaders come to the serving table. Each tears off a piece of the bread. They take it back to their group and take it from person to person, allowing each person to tear off a piece of the bread from the loaf. Do not pass it around. Have the group leader serve each person.*)

Leader: Now, eat your bread, symbolizing His overcoming life in you.

(*Have a moment of silence.*)

Leader: Now we turn our attention to His blood. His blood reminds us that we are saved by His Life. Allow the eyes of your heart to see that He went into the heavenly tabernacle with His own blood and poured it out of His own body, as the blood continues to flow from His beautiful wounds. His blood flows in you. Feel its power.

Leader: As you continue to let the blood flow in you, through you, your group leader will serve you the juice of the vine. As you hold your cup of juice until the appropriate time, let it be a symbol for you of His eternal, cleansing life.

(*Group leaders come to the serving table and pick up a tray of communion cups filled with juice. They take it to their group and hand each one a cup.*)

Leader: Now, drink the cup, remembering that Christ in you is your hope of glory.

(*Have a moment of silence.*)

Leader: Remember that our flesh is a tourniquet that cuts off the flow of His Life. Take a moment to allow the Spirit to speak to you about a tourniquet that He would like to release in your life. When you know exactly what God is saying, and when you can say to Him, "I give you this tourniquet in my life. I let it go. I want all of You flowing through me at full power." When you can say that, write what you are releasing on the slip of paper at your seat.
(*Allow time.*)

Leader: Now, when you are ready, walk up here to the basket on the serving table. Tear your slip of paper up and place it in this basket. Let this act symbolize for you that you are placing this flesh-pattern under His blood. You are letting it come into contact with the antibodies in His blood. The music will continue to play and we will continue to worship.

(*As everyone finishes, ask them to stand and sing together the chorus of "Nothing but the Blood," thinking about every word.*)

(*Close in prayer, then close with "The Spirit's Quiet Whisper."*)

The Spirit's Quiet Whisper

Vocal and Piano

Words by Jennifer Kennedy Dean
and Roxanne Lingle
Music By Roxanne Lingle

Also by Jennifer Kennedy Dean

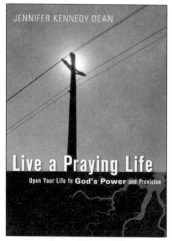

LIVE A PRAYING LIFE
Open Your Life to God's Power
and Provision
1-56309-752-4

LEGACY OF PRAYER
A Spiritual Trust Fund for the
Generations
1-56309-711-7

RICHES STORED IN SECRET PLACES
A Devotional Guide for Those Who
Hunger After the Deep Things of God
1-56309-203-4

THE PRAYING LIFE
Living Beyond Your Limits
1-56309-091-0

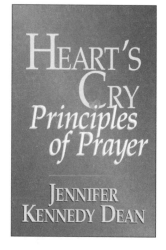

HEART'S CRY
Principles of Prayer
1-56309-047-3

HE RESTORES MY SOUL
A Forty-Day Journey
Toward Personal Renewal
0-80542-027-4

Also

HE LEADS ME BESIDE STILL WATERS
A Forty-Day Journey
Toward Rest for Your Soul
0-80542-379-6

AVAILABLE IN CHRISTIAN BOOKSTORES EVERYWHERE.

New Hope
Publishers

Equipping You to Share the Hope of Christ

To schedule
Jennifer Kennedy Dean
for your event, contact:

The Praying Life Foundation
PO Box 62
Blue Springs, MO 64013
888.844.6647
seminars@prayinglife.org
www.prayinglife.org

Resources for leading the study *The Life-Changing Power in the Blood of Christ* are available at www.prayinglife.org or by calling 888.844.6647.

Leader's Kit contains: (1) video series of Jennifer Kennedy Dean teaching the concepts with a live audience. Each video session is 30-45 minutes in length. The series is available on VHS or DVD; (2) CD of the song "Spirit's Quiet Whisper" referenced in Week 8.

Visit www.prayinglife.org to:

- Find answers to frequently asked questions
- Ask Jennifer your own questions
- Find a monthly column by Jennifer Kennedy Dean
- Discover a wealth of resources for your praying life
- Read doctrinal papers on this book's topics